797,885 Books
are available to read at

www.ForgottenBooks.com

Forgotten Books' App
Available for mobile, tablet & eReader

ISBN 978-1-330-88018-0
PIBN 10116311

This book is a reproduction of an important historical work. Forgotten Books uses state-of-the-art technology to digitally reconstruct the work, preserving the original format whilst repairing imperfections present in the aged copy. In rare cases, an imperfection in the original, such as a blemish or missing page, may be replicated in our edition. We do, however, repair the vast majority of imperfections successfully; any imperfections that remain are intentionally left to preserve the state of such historical works.

Forgotten Books is a registered trademark of FB &c Ltd.
Copyright © 2015 FB &c Ltd.
FB &c Ltd, Dalton House, 60 Windsor Avenue, London, SW19 2RR.
Company number 08720141. Registered in England and Wales.

For support please visit www.forgottenbooks.com

1 MONTH OF FREE READING

at

www.ForgottenBooks.com

By purchasing this book you are eligible for one month membership to ForgottenBooks.com, giving you unlimited access to our entire collection of over 700,000 titles via our web site and mobile apps.

To claim your free month visit:
www.forgottenbooks.com/free116311

* Offer is valid for 45 days from date of purchase. Terms and conditions apply.

Similar Books Are Available from
www.forgottenbooks.com

Travels in the Interior of Africa
by Mungo Park

Via Rhodesia
A Journey Through Southern Africa, by Charlotte Mansfield

A Visit to India, China, and Japan in the Year 1853
by Bayard Taylor

Italian Castles and Country Seats
by Tryphosa Bates Batcheller

Captain Cook's Third and Last Voyage to the Pacific Ocean, Vol. 1 of 4
In the Years 1776, 1777, 1778, 1779 and 1780, by James Cook

Travels in Peru and Mexico
by S. S. Hill

A Handbook for Travellers in Southern Italy
Comprising the Description, by John Murray

The Handbook for Travellers in Spain, Vol. 1
by Richard Ford

A New Collection of Voyages, Discoveries and Travels
by John Adams

The Sacred City of the Ethiopians
Being a Record of Travel and Research in Abyssinia in 1893, by J. Theodore Bent

The Outgoing Turk
Impressions of a Journey Through the Western Balkans, by H. C. Thomson

Travels in the Old World
Illustrated, by J. M. Rowland

The Travels of Marco Polo, the Venetian
The Translation of Marsden Revised, by Marco Polo

Travels in Arabia
by Bayard Taylor

From the Gulf to Ararat, an Expedition Through Mesopotamia and Kurdistan
by G. E. Hubbard

From Occident to Orient and Around the World
by Charlton B. Perkins

The Periplus of the Erythræan Sea
Travel and Trade in the Indian Ocean By a Merchant of the First Century, by Wilfred H. Schoff

Five Years in a Persian Town
by Napier Malcolm

Central Asia, Travels in Cashmere, Little Tibet, and Central Asia
by Bayard Taylor

The Bondage and Travels of Johann Schiltberger
A Native, by Johannes Schiltberger

THE

KINGDOM OF GEORGIA

*NOTES OF TRAVEL IN A LAND OF WOMEN
WINE, AND SONG*

TO WHICH ARE APPENDED HISTORICAL, LITERARY, AND
POLITICAL SKETCHES, SPECIMENS OF THE NATIONAL
MUSIC, AND A COMPENDIOUS BIBLIOGRAPHY

By OLIVER WARDROP

WITH ILLUSTRATIONS AND MAPS

LONDON
SAMPSON LOW, MARSTON, SEARLE, & RIVINGTON

LONDON:
PRINTED BY GILBERT AND RIVINGTON, LIMITED,
ST. JOHN'S HOUSE CLERKENWELL ROAD.

TO

PROFESSOR JAMES BRYCE, M.P.,

𝕴𝖍𝖊𝖘𝖊 𝕹𝖔𝖙𝖊𝖘 𝖆𝖗𝖊 𝕯𝖊𝖉𝖎𝖈𝖆𝖙𝖊𝖉

(*By permission*),

WITH HEARTFELT GRATITUDE AND PROFOUND RESPECT.

593806

PREFACE.

There were four of us—two Frenchmen, an Italian, and an Englishman. We had ridden from Damascus to Baalbek, and had seen the ruins; after dinner, we were lying on heaps of cushions on the floor, in a hostelry little known to Europeans. For some minutes the bubbling of our narghilés was the only sound that broke the stillness of the night. Then the ex-cuirassier spoke out in a strong voice—the voice of a man accustomed to command—"Gentlemen! I propose that we solemnly pass a vote of censure on the late M. de Lamartine." "Bravo!" was our unanimous cry; and the vote was carried, *nemine contradicente*. A rider was added, to the effect that poets should be discouraged from writing books of travel.

"Surely a strange proceeding!" says the

reader. Let me explain. We had been shut up in Damascus for a long time by heavy snow-storms which blocked the roads; the most interesting book we had was Lamartine's "Voyage en Orient," and we had read the long description of Baalbek over and over again, until we almost knew it by heart. Need I say that the reality disappointed us? If we had never read Lamartine's book, we should have been delighted with the place; but having read it, we wanted the poet's eyes in order to see the temples as he saw them.

But what has all this to do with Georgia? Simply this: the following pages are not written by a poet, and, gentle sir, if you ever pass a vote of censure on the writer of them, it will not be for the reason that he has painted things and places in a rose-coloured atmosphere.

In publishing these notes I have had but one object—to excite the curiosity of my fellow countrymen; the means of gratifying this curiosity are indicated in the bibliographical section. Georgia is practically unknown to the British public; well-educated people know that the country is famous for its beautiful women, but they are not very sure whether those charming creatures live under Persian, Turkish, or Russian rule, while not one person in a thousand knows that the Georgians and Circassians are distinct peoples.

If you suggest that Transcaucasia is a good place for a holiday, you meet with a look of blank astonishment—it is just as if you had said the Sooloo Islands, or Vladivostok. When you explain that Georgia is now a part of the Russian Empire, you hear stereotyped remarks about police and passports. The intending visitor need have no anxiety on this score; even in Moscow a foreigner is seldom or never put to any inconvenience, in the Caucasus he almost forgets that he has such a thing as a passport.

There is no reason why Georgia should not become as popular a resort as Norway or Switzerland. It is not so far away as people imagine— you can go from London to Tiflis, overland, in a week; it is at least as beautiful as either of the countries just named; it has the great advantage of being almost unknown to tourists; there is none of the impudent extortion which ruffles our tempers nearer home, and it is, after all, a cheaper place to travel in than Scotland. All these circumstances ought to have an influence on the holiday-maker in search of health and recreation.

The botanist, the geologist, the archæologist, the philologist will all find there mines of rich materials yet unknown to their respective sciences. The mountaineer knows the country already, through Mr. Freshfield's excellent book; the sportsman knows it too, thanks to Mr. Wolley. Artists will get there a new field for the brush, the pencil, and the camera. But, after all, Georgia's chief attraction lies in its people; the Georgians are not only fair to look upon, but they are essentially a lovable people; it is a true proverb that says, "The Armenian's soul is in his head, the Georgian's in his eyes;" to live among such gay, open-hearted, open-handed, honest, innocent folk is the best cure for melancholy and misanthropy that could well be imagined.

The language will occur to most people as a difficulty. Either Russian or Georgian carries the traveller from the Black Sea to the Caspian, even Turkish is pretty well known; in the larger towns one can always find hotels where French or German is understood, and where interpreters can be hired. Those who have travelled know that a very slight knowledge of a language is sufficient for all practical purposes, and such a knowledge of Georgian could be picked up in a week or so; Russian is more difficult, both in grammar and pronunciation. It may be a consolation to some, to know that a lady, Mme. Carla Serena, who travelled alone, and spent a long time in the wildest part of the Caucasus, could not speak a dozen words of Russian or Georgian.

Let me clearly repeat what I said in the first paragraphs of this preface : in the following plain, matter-of-fact record of travel my aim has not been to give immediate pleasure, but rather to show how and where pleasure may be obtained. Autumn is the best season for a visit, and spring is the next best time.

My hearty thanks are due to Mr. W. R. Morfill, for his kindness in reading through the chapters on the history and literature of Georgia.

O. W.

Oxford, September, 1888.

NOTE.

In transcribing proper names I have tried to preserve the original orthography as far as possible.

a should be pronounced as in f*a*ther.
e   ,,   ,,   like *a* in m*a*de.
i   as in mach*i*ne.
u   as in r*u*de.
ch   as in *ch*urch.
kh   like *ch* in Scottish and German.
s   as in *s*un.
z   as in ama*z*e.
g   as in *g*un.
y   as in *y*ellow.

CONTENTS.

	PAGE
BATUM TO TIFLIS	1
TIFLIS	8
THE GEORGIAN MILITARY ROAD BETWEEN TIFLIS AND VLADIKAVKAZ	34
THE KAKHETIAN ROAD—TIFLIS TO SIGNAKH	69
SIGNAKH	78
A TRIP ACROSS THE ALAZANA	83
SIGNAKH TO TELAV, AND THENCE TO TIFLIS	100
THE HISTORY OF GEORGIA	113
THE LANGUAGE AND LITERATURE OF GEORGIA	136
THE POLITICAL CONDITION OF THE KINGDOM OF GEORGIA	155

APPENDIX.

BIBLIOGRAPHY	171
STATISTICS	197
SPECIMENS OF GEORGIAN VOCAL MUSIC	201

LIST OF ILLUSTRATIONS.

Tiflis	*Frontispiece*
Maps of Transcaucasian Railway and Military Road	*To face page* 1
A Georgian Wrestler	,, 30
Saint Nina	40
Ananur	46
Dariel Fort and Ruins of Tamara's Castle	62
Dariel	64
Vladikavkaz	66
An Arba	73
A Street in Signakh	80
Georgian National Costume	84
The City Wall, Telav	,, 108
Queen Tamara	,, 114
Irakli II.	,, 124
Rustaveli	,, 139
Prince Ilia Chavchavadze	,, 150
Prince Ivané Machabeli	,, 153
Bishop Gabriel of Kutaïs	,, 154
Map of Georgia	*At the end.*

UNIV. OF
CALIFORNIA

TRANSCAUCASIAN RAILWAY. GEORGIAN MILITARY ROAD.

G. Philip & Son, London and Liverpool

To face p. 1.

THE KINGDOM OF GEORGIA.

BATUM TO TIFLIS.

ONE morning in April, 1887, after a five days' passage from Odessa, we entered the harbour at Batum.

Batum (Hôtel Imperial, Hôtel de France, Hôtel d'Europe) is a town of 10,000 inhabitants, mostly Georgians; it consists of an ancient Asiatic quarter, dirty and tumble-down looking, and a European one only seven years old. Its situation at the foot of the mountains is lovely beyond all description. The place has a decidedly "Far West" look about it, everything seems half-finished; the streets are broad and, with a few exceptions, unpaved, the depth of the mud varies from three or four inches to half a yard, heaps of rotting filth furnish food for numerous pigs, and in the best thoroughfares ducks find convenient lakes on which to disport themselves.

I took an early opportunity of presenting myself at the British Vice-Consulate, a small, two-storey cottage, the lower half of which is of brick, the upper of corrugated iron sheets. Mr. Demetrius R. Peacock, the only representative of British interests in the Caucasus, is a man whose services deserve fuller recognition. It would be hard to find a post where more diplomatic tact is required, yet he contrives to make himself respected and admired by all the many races with which he is in daily contact. Mr. Peacock was born in Russia, and has spent most of his life in that empire, but he is nevertheless a thorough Englishman. In Tiflis I heard a good story about him. On one occasion the French Consul-General jokingly said to him, " Why, Peacock, you are no Englishman, you were born in Russia." To which our representative replied, " Our Saviour was born in a stable, but for all that He did not turn out a horse."

Although Batum is not very attractive as a town, it is at any rate far preferable to Poti or Sukhum, and it has undoubtedly a splendid future before it. Even at the present time the exports amount to nearly 400,000 tons, chiefly petroleum, manganese ores, wool, cotton, maize, tobacco, wine, fancy woods, &c. It is essentially a city of the future; and its inhabitants firmly believe that it will yet be a powerful rival of Odessa in trade, and of the Crimean coast-towns as a watering-place. At present we should hardly recommend it to invalids; the marshes round about are gradually being drained; but they still produce enough malaria to make the place dangerous to Europeans; the drinking-water, too, is bad.

The harbour is fairly well sheltered, but rather small; yet, to the unprofessional eye, there seems no reason why it might not easily be enlarged if necessary. The entrance is protected by a fortification in the form of an irregular rectangle, lying on the S.W. corner of the bay, behind the lighthouse. The earthworks, about seventy or eighty feet high, and lined with masonry, cover a piece of ground apparently about 300 paces long by 180 paces broad; a broad-gauge railway surrounds the fortress. When I was there the work was being pushed forward very rapidly, and preparations were being made to fix a heavy gun close to the lighthouse—at that time there were only about a dozen guns of small calibre in position.

In the town there is absolutely nothing to attract the stranger's attention; a few mosques and churches, petroleum refineries, half a dozen European shops, some half-finished public buildings, and the embryo of a public garden on the shore serve as an excuse for a walk; but if the traveller happens to hit upon a spell of wet weather, he will soon have seen all he wants to see of Batum, and will get out of its atmosphere of marsh gas and petroleum as soon as possible.

The only daily train leaves at eight o'clock in the morning; the station, although it is a terminus of so much importance, is a wretched wooden building, a striking contrast to the one at Baku, which would not disgrace our own metropolis. The railway skirts the sea for about thirty miles, and on the right lies a range of hills covered with a luxuriant growth of fine forest-trees and thick undergrowth gay with blossoms; in the neighbourhood of the town there are already many pretty villas. The rain of the previous few weeks had made the woods wonderfully beautiful, and the moist air was heavy with fragrance; I never saw such a wealth of plant life before. At Samtredi, where the lines from Batum and Poti meet, we leave Guri and Mingreli behind us and enter Imereti. On the left we now have a fine broad plain, and near us flows the Rion, the ancient Phasis. The country is far more thickly populated than Guri or Mingreli, or any other part of Trans-Caucasia, but it could easily support a much larger number if the ground were properly worked. I was amazed when I saw, for the first time, five pairs of oxen dragging one wooden plough, but the sight of this became familiar to me before I had lived long in Georgia. At the roadside stations (I need hardly say that our train stopped at all of them) I saw some fine faces—one poor fellow in a ragged sheepskin cloak quite startled me by his resemblance to Dante Alighieri. From the station of Rion, on the river of that name, a branch line runs northward to Kutaïs, none other than the Cyta in Colchis whence Jason carried off Medea and the Golden Fleece.

Kutaïs (Hôtel de France, Hôtel Colchide, Hôtel d'Italie) is a beautiful town of 25,000 inhabitants, almost all Georgians. The ruins of an old castle on the other side of the river show where the town stood a century ago, and from this point the best view of Kutaïs is obtained. Abundance of good building-stone, a rich soil, and plenty of trees, render the capital of Imereti a charming sight; its elevation of about 500 feet makes its atmosphere cool and bracing compared with that of the coast-towns. The traveller who wishes to become acquainted with Georgian town-life cannot do better than stay in Kutaïs a month or two.

About five miles off is the monastery of Gelati, built in the tenth century, and renowned as the burial-place of the glorious Queen Tamara. From Kutaïs a journey may be made to Svaneti, the last Caucasian state conquered by Russia, and even now only nominally a part of the Tsar's dominions; Mr. Wolley's book, " Savage Svanetia," will give the intending visitor some idea of the sport that may be had in that wild region. The road across the Caucasus from Kutaïs to Vladikavkaz is much higher and wilder than the famous Dariel road, and I much regret that I had not time to travel by it.

Pursuing our journey from Rion to the eastward we soon reach Kvirili, which is about to be connected by a branch line of railway with Chiaturi, the centre of the manganese district; at present all the ore is carried down to the main line, a distance of twenty-five miles, in the wooden carts called *arbas*. Passing through glens of wondrous beauty, adorned with picturesque ruins of ancient strongholds, we at length arrive at the mountain of Suram, 3027 feet above Black Sea level, the watershed which separates the valley of the Kura, with its hot summers and cold winters, from the more temperate region drained by the Rion. The railway climbs very rapidly to the summit of the pass, but it comes down still more rapidly; there is a slope of one in twenty for a distance of a thousand feet; at the bottom is the town of Suram with its fine old castle. We now follow the course of the Kura all the way to Tiflis, passing Mikhailovo (whence a road runs to Borzhom, the most fashionable summer-resort in Trans-Caucasia) and Gori, a good-sized town, near which is the rock city of Uphlis Tsikhe. It is half past nine at night before Mtzkhet, the ancient capital of Georgia, is reached, and at a quarter past ten we enter Tiflis, ten hours from Kutaïs, and fourteen hours from Batum. Our journey is not yet ended, however, for it takes half an hour to drive from the station to the fashionable quarter of the town where the hotels are situated.

TIFLIS.

The best hotels are Kavkaz, Rossiya, London; all pretty good. If the traveller intends to make a prolonged stay, he can easily find furnished apartments and dine at a restaurant (e g. the French Restaurant d'Europe, opposite the Palace). The best plan of all is to board with a Georgian family; but without good introductions it is somewhat difficult to do this. Although beef only costs $1\frac{1}{2}d.$ a pound and chickens $2d.$ each, living is dear in Tiflis; the necessaries of life, except house-rent and clothing, are cheap, and one need not, like Alexandre Dumas, pay three roubles for having his hair cut, but the "extras" are heavy, and if the visitor is not disposed to spend his roubles with a free hand and a light heart, he will meet with a poor reception, for the Georgian hates nothing more than meanness, a vice from which he firmly believes Englishmen to be free.

Tiflis takes its name from the hot medicinal springs, for which it has been famous for fourteen centuries at least; in Georgian it is called Tphilisi, which philologists assert to be derived from a root akin to or identical with the Indo-European *tep;*

the meaning of Toeplitz and Tiflis is thus the same. In the fifth century king Vakhtang Gurgaslan founded Tiflis, and began to build the Cathedral of Sion, which still stands in the midst of the city. The castle, situated on a high, steep rock, near the Kura, is older than the city itself, and its construction is attributed to the Persians. Tiflis has shared in all the triumphs and misfortunes which have befallen Georgia, and the history of the capital would only be a repetition of the history of the nation.

The city is built on both sides of the Kura, at an elevation of 1200 feet, between two ranges of steep, bare hills, which rise to a height of 2500 feet, and hem it in on all sides, thus it lies at the bottom of a deep rock basin, and this accounts for the terrible heat which renders it such an unpleasant dwelling-place in July and August. The river Kura is crossed by several fine bridges, the best of which is named after Prince Vorontsov, who during his governorship did great things for Trans-Caucasia, and gained for himself the lasting gratitude of all the peoples committed to his care. The population of 105,000 consists not only of Georgians, but of Russians (civil servants and soldiers), Armenians (traders and money-lenders), Persians, Tatars, and a few Europeans, viz. Germans (colonists from Suabia), Frenchmen (milliners, hotel-keepers), &c. Although the English residents might be counted on one's fingers, it seems a pity that her Majesty's Consulate should have been closed in 1881; surely Great Britain has in Georgia interests at least equal to those of France, Germany, Belgium, and the other nations which have representatives in Tiflis.

The effect which Tiflis produces on the mind of the stranger is perfectly unique; its position, its surroundings, the varied nature of its street-life, the gaiety and simplicity of its social life, all combine to form a most powerful and most pleasurable impression. If the reader will mentally accompany me, I shall take him through some of the more interesting quarters, and endeavour to give him some idea of the place. First of all, starting from the fashionable district called Salalaki, let us climb the rocky road which leads to the ruins of the castle, whence we obtain the finest view of the city. The best time to enjoy the panorama is evening, and in summer no one would ever think of making the toilsome ascent much before sunset. From these crumbling walls one looks over a vast expanse of house-tops and church spires, through the midst of which winds the muddy Kura. At our feet lies the old town, a labyrinth of narrow, crooked streets, stretching from the square of Erivan down to the waterside, where stands the Cathedral of Sion. Quite near at hand the river becomes very narrow, and advantage of this circumstance has been taken by building a bridge, which leads to the citadel of Metekh (now used as a prison) and the large Asiatic quarter called Avlabar. On this side of the river, forming a continuation of the range of hills on which we are standing, rises the Holy Mount (Mtatsminda), and perched high up near its summit is the pretty white church of St. David, behind which rises a wall of bare, black rock; half-way between it and the river is the Governor's palace, with its extensive gardens, just at the beginning of the Golovinskii Prospekt, a long boulevard with fine shops and public buildings; between the boulevard and the river lies the Municipal Garden, named after Alexander I. Turning our eyes towards the other side of the Kura, beyond Avlabar, we see, on the hill facing St. David's, a large block of buildings used as a military depôt, arsenal, and barracks, and still farther on, on the river bank, is a thick green belt which we recognize as the gardens of Mikhailovskaya Street, ending in the splendid park called Mushtaïd. Crossing the ridge, we now turn our back on the city and descend into the Botanical Garden, situated in a sheltered ravine, a delightful place for an evening stroll; on the opposite side of the ravine is a Tatar village with a lonely graveyard.

The Erivan Square is the great centre of activity; in its midst is the Caravanserai, a vast rectangular building full of shops, not unlike the Gostinoï Dvor, in Petersburg, but poorer. From that corner of the square in which is the Hôtel du Caucase, runs Palace Street, all one side of which is occupied by the Caravanserai of the late Mr. Artsruni, a wealthy Armenian, and behind, in a fine garden, is the Georgian theatre; both the garden and the theatre belong to the Land Bank of the Nobles, an institution which deserves the attention of all who are interested in the Iverian nation. The bank was founded in 1874 in order to aid farmers to work their lands by advancing them money at the lowest possible rate of interest; all the profits are spent in the furtherance of philanthropic schemes and in the encouragement of national education. It is a significant fact that the more intelligent members of Georgian society should have chosen this mode of activity in preference to any other, but the reason of their choice is apparent; from the bitter experience of the last hundred years they have learnt that although munificence is one of the noblest of the virtues, extravagance and ostentation are hurtful, and they have, therefore, wisely determined to do all they can to improve the economic condition of the country. The public meetings of the shareholders give an opportunity for discussion and speech-making, and it is in this "Gruzinskii Parlament" (as the Russians have nicknamed it) that Prince Chavchavadze has gained for himself the not un-merited title of the "Georgian Gambetta." I was an occupant of the Ladies' Gallery at one of these assemblies, and I shall never forget the impression produced upon me by the sight of these handsome, warlike Asians in their picturesque garb, conducting their proceedings exactly in the same order as British investors do every day in the City of London. Try and imagine the heroes of the Elizabethan Age at Cannon Street Hotel discussing the current dividend of the S.E.R., and you will have some idea of my feelings.

Only those who have lived the life of the people in Trans-Caucasia know what a terrible curse the money-lending community are. A local proverb says, "A Greek will cheat three Jews, but an Armenian will cheat three Greeks," and the

Georgian, straightforward, honest fellow, is but too often cruelly swindled by the artful children of Haïk. When the fraud is very apparent the Armenian often pays for his greed with all the blood that can be extracted from his jugular vein. During my stay in Tiflis, a certain wild young prince, Avalov, had made himself popular by slaughtering a few Armenians; his latest exploit made so much stir that a prosecution was talked of; but Avalov was no dweller in towns, he spent his time merrily out in the greenwood, and it would have needed a company of Kazaks to arrest him. While the authorities were deliberating, the prince sent a polite message to say that if they tried to make matters unpleasant for him, he would, with God's help, devote the remainder of his natural life to running amuck of every "salted" Armenian (a reference to their habit of salting children as soon as they are born) that crossed his path. Another young nobleman got three years' imprisonment for "perforating" an insulting usurer, and the cruelty of the sentence was much spoken of; a lady said to me, "Just fancy, that fine young fellow imprisoned among common criminals for killing a rascal of an Armenian," as who should say for killing a dog.

Let it be clearly understood that I say nothing

against the Armenian nation; I have the strongest admiration for their undoubted literary and administrative talent, and for the energy with which they resist all attempts to destroy their national spirit. The Armenian not being a money-lender or trader, is a citizen of which any country might be proud; but the usurer, whether he be Jew, Armenian, or Briton, is a most despicable character, and, unfortunately, the peculiar conditions under which the Armenians have lived for many centuries have necessarily made Shylocks of a large percentage of them.

Continuing our walk, we emerge from Palace Street into the wide Golovinskii Prospekt, which takes its name from Golovin, a former governor of the Caucasus. On the left lies the palace, a fine modern building in the European style, and on the right is the Caucasian Museum, in which the student will find geological, zoological, ethnographical, entomological, botanical, archeological, and numismatic collections of the highest interest. On the walls of the staircase are several large pictures, the most interesting of which are, a portrait of Queen Tamara, copied from the painting at Gelati, and " The Arrival of the Argonauts in Colchis," the figures in which are all portraits, the Grand Duke Nicholas Mikhailovich being represented as Jason. There is also a very large collection of photographs, comprising all that is worth seeing in the Caucasus and in Persia. In the same block of buildings is the Public Library, in which will be found most of the literature relating to the country, and a fair number of books on general subjects.

The library is at the corner of the Prospekt and Baronovskaya Street, and turning down the latter, the first turning on the right brings us to the Post Office, facing which is a girls' grammar school. The traveller who happens to pass that way when the lessons for the day are over (and he might do worse if he likes to see pretty young faces), will be surprised, unless he has been in Russia, to see that all the children are dressed alike, regardless of age, complexion, and taste; he will be still more surprised when he hears that if one of these uniforms is seen out after 5 p.m., the fair wearer is severely punished, it being the opinion of the Tsar's Minister of Education that school-girls, and school-boys too, should after that hour be at home preparing their tasks for next day. The school accommodation is lamentably inadequate; in the government of Tiflis there are only about 280 children at school for every 10,000 of the population, in the government of Kutaïs only 250.

Returning to Golovinskii Prospekt, we pass on the right the Staff Headquarters of the army of the Caucasus, the best restaurant in the city, some good shops, and then arrive at the Aleksandrovskii Garden, which slopes down to the river bank; its shady walks are thronged every evening when a military band performs. Near its extreme corner, and almost on the waterside, is the Russian theatre; although the house is a small one and only used as a makeshift until the new theatre is finished, it is a very pleasant place to spend an evening; good companies from Petersburg and Moscow play during the season, and I saw some of the stars of the profession there. Unfortunately, there is a preference for translations of French and German pieces with which the European is already familiar, but Russian plays are not totally ignored. I once saw a version of " Le Monde où l'on s'ennuie" which was in the smallest details of gesture and property a photographic reproduction of the comedy as I have seen it on the classic boards of the Théâtre Français—but there was one startling innovation, Bellac was described on the programme as an *abbé* (sic!). The great charm of the Tifliskii Theatre is, however, its open air crush-room, a fine large garden where a band plays between the acts, and where refreshments may be partaken of and smoking indulged in.

The new theatre on Golovinskii Prospekt is a handsome edifice which was still unfinished at the time of my visit. The farther you get from the Erivan Square the less aristocratic does the Boulevard become, the only other building of note in that part of it being the Cadets' College; the opening of the new theatre will, however, make a great difference, and in a few years the dirty little beershops on the left will doubtless disappear, and Golovinskii Prospekt will be one of the finest streets in the world. Its situation is a splendid one, and is not unworthy of comparison with that of Princes' Street, Edinburgh; the Holy Mount, rising black and steep to a considerable height, and adorned with the pretty white church of St. David, might not inaptly be said to be to Tiflis what the Castle Hill is to the modern Athens. At the end of the Boulevard is the posting-station, whence we can return to our starting-place by tram-car. All the main thoroughfares of the city are now laid with tram-lines, the construction of which is due to a Belgian company which is paying very good dividends.

Thursday afternoon is the best time for visiting the Church of St. David, for a service is then held and large numbers of women attend. Proceeding from Salalaki along Laboratornaya, which is parallel to the Boulevard and is the most select street in Tiflis, we reach the street of the Holy Mount (Mtatsmindskaya), a steep, roughly-paved thoroughfare which leads up to St. David's Place, and a winding mountain path takes us thence to the church. St. David was a Syrian monk who came to Georgia in the sixth century, and lived a hermit's life among the woods which at that time covered the hill. Tradition says that the daughter of a wealthy man who lived near there, finding herself in an interesting condition, thought the best way of getting out of the difficulty would be to accuse the saint of being the cause of this state of affairs. The holy man, naturally, objected, and having made his accuser appear in an assembly of the people, he proved his innocence by making the unborn child say audibly who was its father. Whereupon, in answer to the prayers of the saint, the child was converted into a stone, which the damsel brought forth immediately. This stone was made the foundation of a church. David then asked that a spring of living water of fructifying virtue might be made to flow; this fountain is still visible, and its water is largely used by married ladies; the climb of twenty minutes from St. David's Place is so toilsome that even the most bitter Malthusian would hasten to quench his thirst there; as far as I know, it is the only water in Tiflis fit for human consumption. Every pious lady who visits the shrine carries a stone or brick up the hill with her, and it is from these that the church was built and is still kept in repair. There is another interesting custom in which maidens and matrons alike take part; after adoring the picture of the Virgin, the suppliant silently walks round the building three times, unwinding as she goes a reel of thread, fit symbol of the boundlessness of her love and veneration for the Immaculate Mother of God. Then picking up one of the pebbles with which the ground is covered, she rubs it against the plastered wall, and with beating heart waits to see if it will stick—if it does, then her prayer has been heard, the lass will have a sweetheart, the wife will have a son. The church is of modern construction, but its design differs in no respect from the ancient Byzantine style, specimens of which may be seen all over Georgia. The interior is like that of any other Greek church, and on the walls there are some quaint but rather crude pictures. The mass is, of course, in Georgian, and the choral service strikes rather strangely on Western ears, although not wanting in melody.

Just below the church is a monument bearing the inscription in Russian : " Aleksandr Sergeyevich Griboyedov, born January 4th, 1795, killed in Teheran, January 30th, 1829. Thy mind and thy deeds will never die in the memory of Russia, but why did my love outlive thee?" The story of Griboyedov's life is a sad but interesting one. By birth, education, and talents he was fitted to become one of the most brilliant members of Russian society, but he was early infected with the restless critical spirit of the century, and at the age of seventeen he had already thought out the plot of his great comedy *Goré ot uma*, which is a bitter satire on · the fashionable life of his day. In 1812 his patriotism led him to join in the national defence, but he never saw active service; like his brother officers he enlivened the monotony of barrack life with the wildest dissipation and folly; for instance, we read that he galloped up two flights of stairs and into a ball-room, that he took advantage of his position as organist in a Polish church, to strike up a well-known comical tune in the midst of high mass. But he soon abandoned this unsatisfactory life, went to Petersburg in 1815, turned his attention to dramatic literature, and produced some successful pieces. In 1818 we find him in Persia as secretary to the embassy at Tavriz; there he led a solitary life and studied the Persian language, he read all the poetical literature of the country, and himself wrote Persian lyrics. In 1823 he took a year's leave of absence, and employed much of the time in revising his great work; it was his aim to make his verse "as smooth as glass," and he sometimes re-wrote a phrase a dozen times before it pleased him. When it was at length finished, the severe censure prevented its representation, and it was many years after the poet's death before the full text of the play was heard in Russia. After taking part in a war against the Caucasian Mountaineers, the Persian war gave him an opportunity of exhibiting a bravery bordering on recklessness, and when Erivan had been stormed it was through his skilful diplomacy that Russia obtained such favourable terms of peace, although the British Minister aided Persia with his counsels. In 1828 he left Petersburg with the rank of ambassador at the Persian Court. Before leaving he expressed to his friends the most gloomy forebodings, he

was sure that he would not return to Russia alive.
At Tiflis, however, he found temporary relief
from his mournful feelings in the society of Nina
Chavchavadze, daughter of Prince Alexander
Chavchavadze, the poet, a lady whom he described
as a "very Madonna of Murillo;" he married
her, and she went with him as far as Tavriz, he
promising to come back to her as soon as possible.
He had no sooner reached Teheran, than his
enemies at the court of the Shah began to excite
popular feeling against him, and an incident soon
occurred which gave some excuse for an attack
on the embassy. An Armenian prisoner who
had risen to the dignity of chief eunuch in the
Shah's household, and two women, an Armenian
and a German, from the harem of a powerful
personage, fled to the Russian ambassador and
asked him to assist them to return to Russian
territory. Griboyedov insisted that, according
to the treaty of peace, all prisoners had a right
to freedom, and he refused to give up the re-
fugees. On the 30th of January, 1829, a mad
yelling crowd of 100,000 men made an attack on
the embassy. Griboyedov, sword in hand, led
out his handful of horsemen and was immediately
killed; only one member of the embassy escaped
death. It was Griboyedov's wish that he should

be buried in Georgia, and they chose this romantic spot which the poet had loved so much during his stay in Tiflis. The beautiful Nina remained faithful to her husband's memory, and mourned for him eight-and-twenty years, until she was carried up the winding path to share his grave.

The view from the churchyard is a splendid one; the whole city, with its wonderful diversity of form and colour, lies at your feet; on the right you can see far along the Kakhetian road, and on the left the great highway to Vladikavkaz follows the winding course of the Kura. In the evening we often climbed to the top of a bare crag not far from the church, carrying with us a large earthenware flagon of wine, a roast leg of mutton, fruit, cucumbers, and other delicacies, and spreading out our cloaks on the ground lay there making merry, singing and telling tales until long after midnight; the lights of the town below us seemed like a reflection of the bright stars above us, and the music and laughter of many a jovial group came up the hillside to mingle with our own.

After descending the hill, we cross the Boulevard at the publishing office of *Kavkaz*, the official organ, and skirting the Alexandrovskii

Garden, soon reach the finest bridge in the town, Vorontsovskii Most, from which we get an interesting view of the waterside part of the Asiatic quarter; most of the houses have balconies overhanging the river, and one is involuntarily reminded of the Tiber banks at Rome. On the other side of the bridge, in a small square, is a statue of Prince Vorontsov, Governor of the Caucasus, from 1844 to 1854. During my stay the good people of that district were astonished one morning to see the Prince's head surmounted by a tall, well-worn sheepskin hat, such as the Lesghians wear; the effect was exceedingly ridiculous, and the youthful revellers who, at considerable risk of breaking their necks, were the authors of the joke, were well rewarded for their pains by the laughter of all who passed that way, for your Georgian is a merry fellow.

Turning to the right, we traverse Peski, a quarter very different from Salalaki. Here we see small open-fronted Oriental shops in which dark Persians ply their trades, making arms, saddlery, jewellery, selling carpets, and doing a hundred other things all before the eyes of men and in the open air. There is a strange confusion of tongues and dresses; a smart little grammar-school girl rubs shoulders with a veiled Mussulman woman, and occasionally you see the uniform of a Russian officer elbowing his way through a crowd of Lesghians, Armenians, Georgians, Persians; through the midst of all this confusion runs the tram-car. We are not beyond all the influences of civilization, for, besides the tramway, we see on a sign-board the legend " Deiches Bir" (? Deutsches Bier), over the picture of a flowing tankard.

We cross the narrow bridge and pay a visit to the baths. Perhaps the reader knows something of the so-called Turkish bath, and imagines that the baths of Tiflis are of the same sort? There is certainly some similarity between the two, but there are profound differences; the treatment to which the visitor is subjected at a Turkish bath in Constantinople is not to be compared with what the Persian shampooer puts you through in Tiflis. He goes through a whole course of gymnastics with you, during which he jumps on your chest, on the small of your back, doubles you up as if you were a fowl ready for cooking, and, besides removing every particle of your epidermis, performs sundry other experiments at which the novice stares aghast. At the end of it all you make up your mind that it is not so terrible as it looks, and as you feel wonderfully refreshed you resolve to return again before long. The water is of a heat of about 100° Fahr., and is impregnated with sulphur and other substances which give it a healing virtue ; it is to these springs that Tiflis owes its existence, and they have always been of much importance in the daily life of the people. Formerly it used to be the fashion for ladies of rank to hire baths and dressing-rooms for a whole day, spending the time in perfuming themselves, staining their finger tips, dressing the hair, and performing a dozen other ceremonies of the toilette, concluding with dinner, but the growth of European habits has rendered this custom less common.

The Cathedral of Sion is, as we said before, as old as the city itself, but, of course, it has suffered considerably at the hands of destroyers and restorers. Its style is the same as that of all the other churches in Georgia, and it doubtless served as a pattern for most of them. The inside has been tastefully decorated in modern times, and produces a pleasing effect, although it seems small to anybody who is familiar with the cathedrals of Europe. In front of the altar is the Cross of St. Nina, formed of two vine branches bound together with the saint's hair; this cross has always been the most sacred relic in Georgia.

There is also a modest tomb, which contains the body of Prince Tsitsishvili, a Georgian who was appointed Governor of the Caucasus by Alexander I., and who, after a glorious career, was foully murdered outside the walls of Baku by the treacherous khan of that city

From the cathedral the way to the European quarter leads through the so-called Armenian Bazar, one of the most interesting parts of the city. Old arms, coats of mail, helmets and shields, such as are still used by the Khevsurs up in the mountains, silver ornaments and many other interesting trifles, may be purchased here, but nothing of great value is offered for sale, and the jewellery, with the exception of filigree work from Akhaltsikhe (which is hard to get and very expensive) is not very good. On the birthday of the Tsarevich, I was walking down to the cathedral in order to be present at High Mass, when I saw an incident thoroughly characteristic of the arbitrary proceedings of the Russian police. A burly *gorodovoi*, clad in white uniform and fully armed, was forcing the Asiatic shopkeepers in the bazar to close their premises in order to do honour to the son of the autocrat. I remembered how I had seen the Turkish soldiery in Jerusalem perform a similar task a few months before, when the young Prince of Naples entered the Holy City; it is true that the Turks went a step further than the Muscovites, for they drove the people out into the main street, and refused to let them go home until the evening, but the idea was the same in both cases. The best native tailor of Tiflis lives in this neighbourhood, and I had the honour of having a Circassian suit made for me by him; it fitted like a glove. I may say that, although a great many people in Tiflis wear European dress, in the country it is almost unknown. I found that for travelling there is nothing better than the Circassian garb; it stands a great deal of rough usage, and always looks respectable.

Mushtaid is the finest promenade in the city. It is situated at the west end, and is approached by the Mikhailovskaya, a long, straight street, with fine gardens on either side of it. Some of the best restaurants in the city are in these vine-shaded gardens, and one of them is devoted to wrestling matches. It was my good fortune to be present at a famous contest in which the Kakhetian champion, Grdaneli, fought a certain bold Imeretian professor of the fancy art. The performance was highly interesting, and it was gratifying to learn from the bills that the proceeds were to be for the benefit of a young man who wanted to study at Petersburg, but had not the necessary means. The inner ring was formed of country gentlemen and officers, all sitting cross-legged on the ground; behind them, tier above tier, were at least a thousand spectators, breathless with expectation. A primitive band, consisting of a drum and a *zurna* (an instrument which sounds like the bagpipes), played a war-like air, to the sound of which the heroes danced round the arena amid the frantic applause of the crowd. Both men were fine fellows, but Grdaneli was a very Hercules, and withal amiable-looking; he was the favourite, and justified his reputation of being invincible by utterly demolishing the Western man in a very short space of time. Every incident of the battle called forth from the bystanders loud yells of praise and encouragement which might have been heard miles off.

The two best clubs have summer quarters in Mikhailovskaya Street, by the waterside—the *Kruzhok* (near the Vera Bridge) and the *Georgian Club* (nearer Vorontsovskii Bridge); both have concert-rooms and gardens attached to them, and the famous dance called *Lesginka* may be seen there with its accompaniment of hand-clapping. The costumes worn by both sexes are picturesque and rich, and one meets people of all nationalities

A GEORGIAN WRESTLER.

Page 30.

AMPHIBIANS

including political exiles from Poland, Russian officers and officials, German professors and representatives of many other races besides Georgians. All arms must be left at the entrance. Georgian music is very unlike our own, and at first it strikes the European as loud, wild, discordant, positively unpleasant, but when one is accustomed to it, it is very agreeable. Before I had heard many of the national melodies, I was very much astonished when an accomplished lady told me that her reason for preferring the Georgian Club to the Kruzhok was, that at the former Asiatic music was performed; but I can now understand her liking for the music of her country. In the Appendix I have written down a few melodies which will not, I think, grate harshly on English ears.

The beauty of the Georgian women has been called in question by some travellers, but these are nearly all men whose acquaintance with the people has been extremely limited. The favourite observation of these critics is a stereotyped phrase about "undeniably good features, but want of animation." Surely Alexandre Dumas the elder knew a beautiful face when he saw it; he says: "*La Grèce, c'est Galatée encore marbre ; la Géorgie, c'est Galatée devenue femme.*"

Mushtaid, the town garden, owes nearly all its

charms to nature, the walks and open spaces are neatly kept, but nearly the whole area is a forest in the recesses of which we may lie undisturbed for hours, looking down on the turbid waters of Kura and listening to the rustling of the leaves above and around. Every evening its avenues are crowded with carriages and horsemen; beautiful faces, tasteful toilettes, gay uniforms all combine to form a charming picture. Fancy fairs are occasionally held, at which the visitor may mingle with all the social celebrities, lose his money in raffles, buy things he doesn't want—in short enjoy himself just as if he were at home. But I doubt whether many frequenters of bazaars in England have seen such an acrobatic feat as was performed in Mushtaid last summer; an individual in tights hung himself by the neck on the upper end of an inclined wire, stretched over the heads of the spectators, and slid down it at lightning speed, firing half a dozen pistol-shots as he went. No week passes without a popular fête of some kind, for the Georgians are as fond of gaiety as any nation in the world.

From the above brief sketch the reader will see that Tiflis is a city where one can live for a long time without suffering from *ennui*. Although the immediate neighbourhood looks bare and uninviting, there are, within a few miles, many beautiful spots well worth a visit. The climate has been much abused by some writers, and it must be admitted that during the months of July and August the heat is very trying, but in my opinion Tiflis is a healthy place; since the great plague of ninety years ago it has been pretty free from epidemics, and although fever and dysentery kill a good many people every year, the victims are nearly all residents of low-lying parts of the city, where no European would live if he could help it. During the warm weather there are often storms, characterized by all the grandeur that might be expected in a region of great mountains so near the tropics; after one of these the steep streets become foaming torrents. The sheltered position of the city protects it from the terrible gusts of wind which make the plain to the eastward almost uninhabitable, and the storms seldom cause any more serious damage than broken windows and flooded houses. Hitherto all the town water was obtained from the Kura, and delivered to the consumer from bullock-skins, but a well has now been dug a little below St. David's, whence the dwellers on the right bank will get a supply of a liquid which is not tepid, not opaque, not evil-smelling, and not semi-solid.

THE GEORGIAN MILITARY ROAD BETWEEN TIFLIS AND VLADIKAVKAZ.

The part which rivers have played in the history of civilization is well illustrated by this road. The Aragva, flowing southward from Gudaur, and the Terek, running northward from it, have formed the highway along which countless crowds of Asiatics have penetrated into Europe. Between the two streams there is a distance of some ten miles, forming a huge but not insurmountable barrier, the virtual removal of which did not take place until our own times. It was General Yermolov who, in 1824, succeeded in making the road practicable for troops of all kinds; but from the poet Puskhin's "Journey to Erzerum" (1829), we learn that there was still room for improvement. The traveller had to go with a convoy of 500 soldiers and a cannon, he dare not lag behind for fear of the mountaineers, provisions and lodgings were scarce and bad, the roads were impassable for carriages, the rate of speed was sometimes only ten miles a day. When we read Pushkin's account, and the one given by Lermontov, in "A Hero of Our Times," we can only ask ourselves, "What was the road like before Yermolov?"

During the wars with Kasi-mullah and Shamil, it became indispensable to effect great improvements, and, at length, about five-and-twenty years ago, under the governorship of Prince Bariatinskii, the road was finished, and is now one of the finest in the world, besides being one of the highest—the Simplon is only 6147 feet above sea-level, while the Dariel road is nearly 2000 feet higher. The total distance from Tiflis to Vladikavkaz is 126 miles, and the distance can be done comfortably in less than twenty hours. During the summer 1150 horses are kept in readiness at the stations, in the winter the number is reduced by about 300. Two stage coaches start from each end every day, but as they run during the night also, much of the beauty of the scenery is lost by those who avail themselves of this mode of conveyance; besides, it is difficult to get an outside seat unless you book it a long time in advance. It is far better to travel by *troïka*, as you are then free to stop when you like and as long as you like, and you get an uninterrupted view of the country through which you pass.

About the middle of June, having previously obtained a formidable-looking document by which Alexander Alexandrovich, Autocrat of all the Russias, commanded all postmasters to supply me with horses immediately on demand, I set out on my journey over the frosty Caucasus, accompanied by a young Russian friend. The *troïka* had been ordered for four a.m., but, of course, it did not turn up till half-past five. For the information of those who have never been in Russia, I may say that a *troïka* is a team of three horses harnessed abreast in a vehicle of unique construction called a *teliezhka*. The form of the cart is like a longitudinal section of a beer barrel; it is large enough to contain an ordinary travelling trunk; it is of wood, has neither sides nor springs, and there are four wheels; the seat is made by slipping a piece of rope through a couple of rings on either side, and laying your cloak and a pillow on the rope; the driver sits on the front edge of the cart; the whole affair is invariably in the last stage of decay. The shafts are so long that the horses cannot kick the bottom out of the thing, and the horse in the centre has his head swung up in a wooden frame.

The driver is always asleep or drunk, or both, but he never lets the reins fall, and at regular intervals mechanically applies the whip to his steeds; he only wakes up when there is a shaky bridge to cross, and, regardless of the notice " Walking pace!", first crosses himself and commends his soul to the saints, then gallops over the creaking structure at racing speed.

As we clattered down the steep rocky streets which lead to the Boulevard, I had not much time to look round; all my attention was necessary to preserve myself from falling out of the cart, the jolting was terrible. However, by the time we had got to the outskirts of the town the road became much smoother; the driver got down and released the clappers of the bells above the middle horse's head, and we rattled along merrily to the tune of eight miles an hour. Just outside the city an imposing cruciform monument marks the spot where the late Tsar's carriage was overturned without injuring his Majesty. Passing the Sakartvelo Gardens, where the good people of Tiflis often dine in vine-covered bowers by the river-side, we cross the Vera, an important tributary of the Kura, and then enter a broad plain which continues for many miles to the westward.

On the other side of the Kura we see Mushtaid; a little farther on is the pretty German colony of Alexandersdorf, with its poplar avenues, neat houses, and modest little white church. All the German colonies in the Caucasus seem to be exactly alike, and they do not in any respect differ from German villages in the fatherland; the colonists altogether ignore the people of the country in which they have settled, and, although they make a comfortable livelihood, their isolated condition and the absence of all European influence must make their lives very narrow and joyless. Some of these colonies were founded in order to set before the native peasantry examples of good agriculture and farm management, but this worthy object has not been attained, and the Teutons are looked upon with feelings generally of indifference, sometimes of positive ill-will. High on the hills behind the colony stands the white monastery of St. Antony, a favourite place for picnics. In the cliffs on the left of our road are numerous holes, variously conjectured to be troglodyte dwellings (like those at Uphlis Tsikhe), rock tombs, places of refuge in time of war, provision stores, &c. Before us we see the road winding up between the hills in a northerly direction, and after crossing the Transcaucasian railway and then the Kura we arrive at the post-house of Mtzkhet, not far from the village of that name.

Mtzkhet, if we are to believe local traditions, is one of the oldest cities on earth, for the story goes that it was founded by a great-grandson of the patriarch Noah. Be that as it may, there are unmistakable signs that a Greek or Roman town existed here at a remote date, and antiquaries generally agree in identifying Mtzkhet with the Acrostopolis of the Romans, the headquarters of Pompey after he had defeated Mithridates and subdued Iberia and Albania. No better spot could have been chosen, for its position at the junction of the Aragva and the Kura commands the two great roads of the country and makes it the key of Transcaucasia. Mtzkhet, the ancient capital of Georgia, was always a place of much importance in the annals of the kingdom; now it is a wretched village of some hundreds of inhabitants. It was here that St. Nina began her work of converting the nation, and we propose to give a brief account of the legends relating to this event.

Tradition says that at the beginning of our era there lived in Mtzkhet a wealthy Jew named Eleazar, who frequently made journeys to Jerusalem on business. On the occasion of one of these visits he became possessed of the tunic of our Lord, which he brought home with him as a present to his daughter. She, expecting a valuable gift, ran out to meet him, and with an angry expression snatched from his hands the precious relic, of which she little knew the worth; she fell dead on the spot, but no force could take the garment from her hands, so it was buried with her, and from her grave there soon grew up a tall cedar, from the bark of which oozed a fragrant myrrh, which healed the sick. Now about three centuries later, that is in the third century of our era, St. Nina was born in Cappadocia. When she was twelve years of age her parents proceeded to Jerusalem, and gave themselves up to religious work, leaving the maiden under the care of a devout old woman, who taught her to read the Scriptures. Nina was very anxious to learn what had become of Christ's tunic, and said to her teacher, "Tell me, I pray thee, where is that earthly purple of the Son of God now kept?" To which the venerable matron replied that it had been taken to a heathen land called Iveria, far away to the northward, and that it lay buried there in the city of Mtzkhet. One night the Blessed Virgin appeared to the damsel in a dream, and said to her, "Go to the Iverian land, preach the Gospel of the Lord Jesus, and He will reward thee. I will be thy guard and guide," and with these words she handed to her a cross made of vine branches. When Nina awoke and saw in her hands the wondrous cross she wept for joy, and after reverently kissing the holy gift she bound the two loose sticks together with her own long hair. This cross has always been the palladium of Georgia, and is still preserved in the Sion Cathedral at Tiflis. Now it so happened that at this time seven-and-thirty maidens, fleeing from the persecutions of Diocletian, left Jerusalem to spread the good tidings in Armenia; St. Nina went with them as far as Vashgarabada, and then pursued her journey alone. As she was entering the city of Mtzkhet, the king of Georgia, Marian, with all his people, went out to a hill in the neighbourhood to offer human sacrifices to idols, but in answer to her prayer a mighty storm arose and destroyed the images. She took up her abode in a cell in the king's garden, and soon became well-known as a healer of the sick. At length the queen fell ill, and St. Nina, having made her whole in the name of Jesus, converted the Georgian court to Christianity, and in 314 A.D. baptized all the people of the city.

Over the spot in the royal garden where her cell had been, the king built the Samtavr church, which still exists, and lies to the left of the post-road. It was then revealed to St. Nina that the tunic, the object of her search, lay buried under a cedar in the middle of the town; the tree was cut down and the robe was found in the hands of the dead girl. On the spot where the cedar stood King Marian built, in 328, the Cathedral of the Twelve Apostles; the cedar was replaced by a column, and this column is said to drip myrrh occasionally, even in these degenerate days of ours. The sacred garment was preserved in the cathedral until the seventeenth century, when Shah Abbas sent it as a present to the Tsar of Russia, Mikhail Fedorovich. It was solemnly deposited in the Cathedral of the Assumption at Moscow, where I saw it last autumn.

Having evangelized Kartli, St. Nina proceeded to Kakheti, where she met with the same success, and died at Bodbé, near Signakh; her tomb is in a monastery overlooking one of the finest landscapes in all Kakheti.

The Cathedral of the Twelve Apostles is the chief place of interest in Mtzkhet. The original church was of wood, but in 378 it was replaced by a stone edifice, which stood until the invasion of Tamerlane. The existing church was built in the fifteenth century. A stone wall, with ruined towers, encloses a rectangular piece of ground, in which stands the cathedral, a fine building about seventy paces long by twenty-five paces broad. It is in the Byzantine style, and the interior is divided into three parts by two rows of columns. Here lie buried the last kings of Georgia and their families, the patriarchs of the church, and other illustrious persons.

The post-house at Mtzkhet was a pleasant surprise to me, but I found nearly all the stations on this road equally comfortable; in many of them there are bed-rooms, a dining-room, a ladies' room, and one can get white bread and European food. Those who have travelled on post-roads in Russia will readily understand my surprise.

Leaving Mtzkhet, our road follows the Aragva along a smooth valley between forest-clad hills; the scenery reminded me very much of some of the dales of Thelemarken in Norway. The soil is rich and well cultivated, and here, as elsewhere, we saw a whole herd of oxen dragging one wooden plough. This valley is one of the most feverish places on the whole road, and the people attribute this to a yellow weed (*Carlina arcaulis*), of which there is a great abundance; strange to say, other places where the plant flourishes have the same unpleasant reputation for unhealthiness, the explanation is doubtless to be found in the fact that this weed grows best in a damp soil.

Tsilkani is the next station, but there is no village there. While waiting for horses we saw in the yard a camel; there are plenty of these amiable animals in Tiflis, but I did not think they went so far north as the Aragva.

The scenery continues to be of the same character as far as the station of *Dushet*, some distance from the garrison-town of that name, which lies in rectangular regularity on the hillside, like a relief map; it is a place of some military importance on account of its position at the entrance of the narrow part of the valley, but it is as uninteresting as any Russian provincial town. Near it is a lake, said to cover a Caucasian Sodom; the traveller looks at the lake with more attention than he would bestow upon it if it were in Switzerland, for lakes, like waterfalls, are very rare in the Caucasus. Soon after leaving Dushet we climb a rather steep hill—the wilder part of the road is about to begin. On our left is a huge, antique-looking edifice with towers and battlements, which we feel sure has a romantic history, but we are disappointed to learn that the place is only a modern imitation. At a pretty spot on the river-bank near here I met on my return a party of about fifty prisoners on their way to Siberia; they were, as a rule, honest enough looking fellows, and I could not help feeling pity for them when I remembered how many cases I knew of in which innocent men had been ruined in mind and body, by exile for crimes with which they had no connection. The road crosses a range of green hills, and passing through scenery very like that of Kakheti, descends to the Aragva again at Ananur, the most picturesque village on the whole road, although the surrounding landscape is tame compared with that to the northward.

Ananur lies in a pretty little valley, amid well-wooded hills. At the southern end of the village, perched on a rising ground, is a partly ruined wall with towers and battlements, within which are two churches, one of them still used for divine service, the other a mouldering heap of moss-grown stones. The post-house is at the farther end of the village, and while the horses are being changed we have time to return to the ruins, about a quarter of an hour's walk; by the road-side are several little shops in which furs of all the wild animals of the country may be bought for a trifle; there is also a small barrack. We now climb up to the citadel, and as we enter we cannot help thinking of some of the scenes of blood which have taken place here, even as late as a century and a half ago, when Giorgi, the Eristav (or headman) of Aragva, defended the castle against the Eristav of Ksan. When the place had been taken and all the garrison slain, Giorgi and his family fled to the old church, thinking that no Christian would violate the right of sanctuary, but the conqueror heaped up brushwood round the building and burnt it down; only one of the ill-fated family escaped alive.

The door by which we are admitted lies on the side farthest removed from the road; it leads us through a square tower into the citadel proper, which occupied a piece of ground about one hundred paces long and forty paces broad; formerly it used to stretch down to the very bank of the river, where a ruined tower may still be seen. On entering we see immediately on the left the ruined house of the Eristav Giorgi; straight in front of us is a well-preserved tower, on the left of which may be seen the ruins of the old church, on the right is the modern church. The old church is, of course, quite ruined; it is only about five-and-

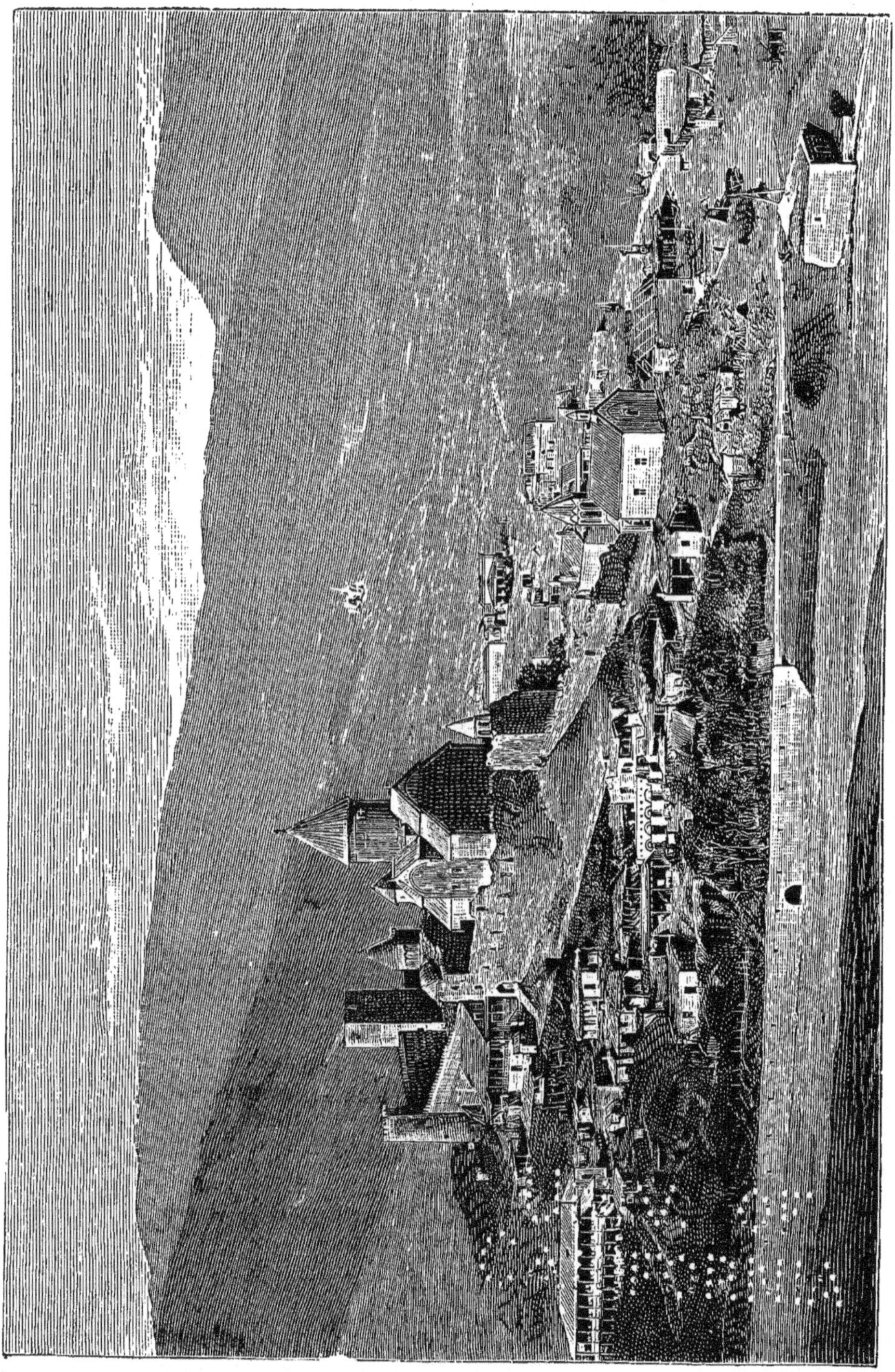

UNIV. OF
CALIFORNIA

twenty paces in length by fifteen paces broad. There still exist fragments of painting and carving which would doubtless prove highly interesting to those who are acquainted with the history of Byzantine art. The building is said to date from the fourth century. There is also a small underground chapel which is fairly well preserved.

The larger church was built by the Eristav Giorgi in 1704; it is thirty paces long by twenty paces broad, and is an enlarged copy of the older sanctuary; the stone of which it is built is yellowish. It is a very fine specimen of Georgian architecture. Beautifully carved in the stone, on each side of the building, is a gigantic cross of vine branches (the cross of St. Nina). The decorative work is excellent throughout, both in design and workmanship; but the figures of animals, &c., are very poor indeed.

Ananur is connected with the darkest page in the mournful latter-day history of Georgia. The Persians had taken Tiflis in 1795, and reduced it to a smouldering heap of ruins. King Irakli, with a few servants, had escaped almost by a miracle, and had taken refuge in the mountain fastness of Ananur; abandoned by his cowardly, faithless children, betrayed by his most trusted dependents and allies, sick in body and weary in mind, the old man of seventy-seven was a sight sad enough to make angels weep. " In the old, half ruined monastery of Ananur, in an ancient cell which used to stand in the corner of the monks' orchard, one have might seen a man dressed in a rough sheepskin cloak, sitting with his face turned to the wall. That man, once the thunderbolt of all Transcaucasia, was the king of Georgia, Irakli II. Near him stood an old Armenian servant. 'Who is that sitting in the corner?' asked those who passed by. 'He whom thou seest,' replied the Armenian, with a sigh, 'was once a man of might, and his name was honoured throughout Asia. His people never had a better ruler. He strove for their welfare like a father, and for forty years kept his empire together; but old age has weakened him, and has brought everything to ruin. In order to prevent quarrels after his death, he determined to divide his kingdom among his children while he still lived, but his hopes in them were deceived. He who was chief eunuch of Tamas Khuli Khan when Irakli was a leader of the Persian army, now marched against him in his feeble old age. His own children refused to help him and their native land, for there were many of them, and each thought he would be striving, not for himself, but for his brother's good. The King of Georgia had to ask the help of the King of Imereti, but if thou hadst been in Tiflis thou hadst seen how shamefully the Imeretians behaved. Irakli, with but a handful of men, fought gallantly against a hundred thousand, and lost his throne only because his children pitilessly forsook him, leaving him to be defeated by a wretched gelding. His ancient glory is darkened, his capital in ruins, the weal of his folk is fled. Under yon crumbling wall thou seest the mighty King of Georgia hiding from the gaze of all men, helpless and clothed in a ragged sheepskin! His courtiers, all those who have eaten his bread and been pressed to his bosom, have left him; not one of them has followed his master, excepting only me—a poor, despised Armenian.'"

From Ananur the road rises along the Aragva valley, which is well cultivated, thanks to a fine system of artificial irrigation. On our left, about a couple of versts from the station, we see high up on a hill the ruined castle and church of Sheupoval, where a grandson of the Eristav Giorgi shared the fate of the rest of his family; the place was burnt down with all its inhabitants. As we pass along the road we meet several pleasant-looking wayfarers, all armed with long, wide dagger, and many carrying in addition sword and rifle; this highway is, however, perfectly safe as far as brigands are concerned, the carrying of weapons is merely a custom which means little more than the use of a walking-stick in our country. Several handsome Ossets, as they pass, courteously salute us with the phrase, "May your path be smooth!" a peculiarly appropriate wish in such a region. When we go through a little village, pretty children run out to look at us, but they never beg, indeed I never saw or heard of a Georgian beggar, although there is much poverty among the people.

All along the road, wherever there is a coign of vantage one sees it topped by the ruins of a four-sided tapering tower, standing in the corner of a square enclosure; every foot of ground has its history of bloodshed and bravery, a history now long forgotten, save for the dim traditions of the peasantry.

The stage between Ananur and Pasanaur (21 versts), is the longest on the whole road, and, although it presents no engineering difficulties such as those which were met with farther to the northward, it is, nevertheless, a toilsome journey for the horses, as it rises about 1300 feet. I shall never forget the pleasant emotions I felt on making the night journey from Pasanaur to Ananur; although there was no moon, the stars shone with a brightness that is unknown in northern latitudes, and lighted up the strange, beautiful landscape; the glittering snow-peaks behind, the silvery stream at our side, the green forests and the lonely ruins made up a picture of surpassing loveliness and weirdness. Fort Gudomakarsk is soon visible, and we know that the station is not far off. I may as well say that almost all the so-called forts between Tiflis and Vladikavkaz are insignificant, neglected-looking places, merely small barracks; they formerly served to keep the mountaineers in order, but now there is really very little necessity for maintaining a garrison in them.

Pasanaur (which in old Persian means "Holy Hill") is situated in a very narrow part of the valley, amid thick woods. The station is a pretty one, and, like that at Ananur, so comfortable that the traveller who has to spend a night there need not be pitied. The only building of interest in the village is a modern church in the Russian style of architecture, which looks as if it had been painted with laundry blue; for ugliness it can compare with any church in Muscovy.

To the eastward of Pasanaur live the Khevsurs,

Pshavs and Tushes, peoples probably having a common origin, and speaking a language akin to Georgian. Their number is variously estimated, from twenty to thirty thousand. They live in a very primitive way, and the Khevsurs still clothe themselves in chain armour and helmets; this circumstance, added to the fact that they have long been Christians, has given rise to the supposition that they are descended from a party of Crusaders who lost their way in trying to return to Europe overland, and settled in these valleys. Their country is among the wildest in the whole range, and their villages are perched high up among the rocks, like eagles' nests. The Khevsurs live chiefly on the scanty products of agriculture; the Pshavs and Tushes are pastoral peoples, in winter they drive their flocks down into Kakheti, and when the snow among the mountains begins to melt they return to their native valleys. All these tribes are wild and brave to the highest degree; from the earliest times they have formed part of the Georgian kingdom, and have distinguished themselves in many a battle against the infidel. The Christianity of this region is not so elaborate as that of Rome or Byzantium, but I suppose it is quite as reasonable as that of the Russian *muzhik* or the English farm-labourer; they have made a saint of Queen Tamara, and they worship the god of war and several other deities in addition to the God Christ. Irakli II. tried to reform their theology, but they replied, "If we, with our present worship, are firm in our obedience and loyalty to the king, what more does he ask of us?" There are now many Orthodox Greek Churches in the villages, but the people totally ignore their existence.

After leaving Pasanaur the road bends to the westward, leaving on the right a high table-shaped mountain of granite which has for a long time seemed to bar our progress; we still keep close to the Aragva, and the scenery becomes bolder, and the soil more barren; here and there we see high up on the face of the rock a cluster of Osset houses; from the valley they look like small dark holes in the cliffs. Pushkin has described them as "swallows' nests," and no happier name could have been chosen.

The Ossets call themselves Ir or Iran, the Tatars and Georgians call them Oss or Ossi. According to official accounts they number over 100,000, about half of them being on each side of the Caucasus. The majority of them profess the Christian religion, but 15,000 are Mahometans, and a considerable number are idolaters. Their traditions say that they came from Asia across the Ural, and used at one time to dwell in the plain to the north of the Caucasus, but were gradually driven into the mountains by stronger peoples. In the reign of Queen Tamara most of them embraced Christianity, and Tamara's second husband was an Osset; they remained tributary to Georgia until the beginning of the present century, and a traveller who visited Tiflis about a hundred years ago says that Irakli's body-guard was composed of Ossets "who never washed." The Ossets were the first Caucasian people to settle down quietly to Russian rule, and they have never given any serious trouble, if we except their share in the Imeretian rising of 1810. The stories about the Ossets being a Teutonic people are as absurd as the assertion that there are in the Crimea Northmen who speak Dutch. They live in a wretched manner, in houses built of loose stones, without mortar; but their physique is good, and their faces are handsome and engaging.

After another long climb of 1300 feet we reach *Mleti*. Here, indeed, we have come to the end of the valley—we are at the bottom of a deep well with sides as bare and steep as walls, on the top glitters the everlasting snow. The engineering difficulties which we have hitherto encountered are as nothing compared with those before us. To our right rises a precipice over three thousand feet high, up which the road climbs in a series of zigzags.

Soon after leaving Mleti we saw the sun set behind the silvery peaks to the west, and within half an hour it was dark; our driver was drunk and fast asleep, and we had occasionally to seize the reins in order to keep the horses from going too near the fenceless edge of the abyss. The distance to Gudaur is only fourteen and a half versts, but nearly the whole ascent has to be done at walking pace; slowly we rose up the hillside, gazing silently now up at the glistening chain above us, now down into the gloomy valley behind us, where a fleecy waterfall shone in the starlight; we saw no wayfarers all the time, and no sound came to break the stillness of the summer night.

At last we reached the tableland at the top, and were soon in the station-house of *Gudaur*, almost 8000 feet above sea-level. Although there were only patches of snow here and there on the ground near us, the air was very cool; only a few days ago we had been simmering in Tiflis in a heat of over 100° Fahr., and now we saw the thermometer down at freezing-point. I knew that as far as comfort went Mleti was a much better place than Gudaur to spend the night at, but I was eager to enjoy the delightful intoxication of the mountain air as soon and as long as possible, and I did enjoy it thoroughly.

After a very rough and hasty supper and a short walk on the edge of the plateau, we entered the common room, and wrapping ourselves up in our *burkas*, sought out the softest plank on the floor, and were soon sleeping the sleep of innocence. Several travellers arrived during the night, for when we rose at dawn we found the room full. Leaving our companions to snore in peace, we ordered the horses, and were soon on our way to the pass.

On the grassy plain were feeding large flocks of goats and sheep, the latter with strange, large, fatty protuberances on either side of the tail. To the right is a remarkable-looking green hill of pyramidal shape, and beyond it an old castle looks down from an inaccessible crag. The scenery of the pass itself is imposing, but it is seen to better advantage when one comes in the opposite direction, i e. from Vladikavkaz to Tiflis; in that case one leaves a scene of the wildest desolation for the luxuriant beauty of the Aragva valley and Kartli; on the northward journey it is, of course, the reverse. The road sinks very rapidly to a depth of almost 2000 feet; the long snow-sheds remind us that even at the present day a winter journey over the Cross Mountain is a serious undertaking; traffic is often stopped for several days at a time by avalanches, and in spring the rivers sometimes wash away the bridges and large pieces of the road. At the foot of the mountain we meet the foaming Terek, a river almost as muddy as the Kura, and following its course reach a vast plain, on the east side of which stands Kobi.

Near *Kobi* station there are two villages; the larger of the two lies under the shadow of a perpendicular rock on the one side on the other side it is flanked by a rugged crag, on the top of which may be seen the ruins of a church and a castle. By the roadside are curious monumental tablets, painted with hieroglyphs of various kinds, among which the rising sun generally occupies the chief place. All round Kobi there are numerous medicinal springs of all kinds, and the station-house is intended to accommodate a few patients. There may come a day when Kobi will be as fashionable as Kissingen, but in the meantime it is not the sort of place that one would recommend to an invalid.

On the score of originality nothing can be said against the environs of Kobi; when we looked round we could not help thinking of the phrase "riddlings of creation," which we have heard applied to the Scottish Highlands; it does, indeed, look as if some of the materials left over after the creation of our earth, had been left here in disordered heaps, to give us some idea of chaos. The road now follows the course of the Terek, and the scenery is indescribably grand; straight before us lies snowy Kazbek in all its rugged wildness, here and there are ruined towers, and about the middle of the stage a turn in the road brings us to an *aul,* or village, of mediæval appearance, by the side of which is a little copse, a rarity in this bleak district. The basaltic rocks present many fantastic shapes and colours to the eye; in several places I saw what looked like huge bundles of rods, reminding me of the Giant's Causeway. Before reaching the station we were met by children who offered for sale all sorts of crystals, pieces of quartz and other pretty geological specimens.

Kazbek station is a very comfortable inn, where one can dine well, and is to be recommended as a place for a prolonged stay. The mountain, generally called Kazbek, rises from the valley in one almost unbroken mass, reaching a height of 16,550 feet above sea-level; the Georgians call it Mkhinvari (ice mountain), and the Ossets, Christ's Peak; Kazbek is really the name of the family who own this part of the country, and is wrongly applied to the mountain. This peak, like Ararat, enjoys the reputation of being inaccessible, and our countrymen, Freshfield, Moore, and Tucker, who climbed to the top, without much difficulty, in June, 1868, were not believed when they told the story of their ascent. On the mountain the sportsman can occasionally get a shot at a *tur* (aurochs, *Ægoceros Pallasii*); but if he is unwilling to expose himself to the necessary danger and fatigue, he can for a few roubles buy a pair of horns at the station.

Those who invade the realm of the mountain spirit should not fail to visit Devdorak glacier, the easiest way of making the ascent; there they will see a place where the native hunters make sacrifices of *tur* horns to propitiate the spirit, who might otherwise throw blocks of ice down on their heads.

There is a popular legend to the effect that on the summit of Mkhinvari is the tent of the

Patriarch Abraham, within which, in a cradle held up by an unseen hand, lies the child Jesus asleep; outside there grows some wheat of wonderful size, beside the tree of life; round the cradle are heaps of treasures. Under the reign of King Irakli II., a priest and his son started for the summit in order to see these wonders; the boy returned alone, bearing samples of the material of the tent, some big grains of wheat, &c., the soles of his boots were covered with silver coins which had stuck to them—unfortunately it was found that the coins were quite modern!

As is well known, Mkhinvari is generally identified with the story of Prometheus, although the mountain does not correspond with the description given by Æschylus. Early travellers even went so far as to assert that they had seen the very chains with which the hero was bound, and there is a local legend to the effect that a giant still lies there in fetters. When I approached the mountain from Kobi I could not help being reminded of Prometheus. I saw a gigantic black space of irregular form with snow all round it; an imaginative mind found in this irregular tract a considerable resemblance to the human shape.

No traveller should leave Kazbek without making a pilgrimage to the monastery of St.

Stephen, which stands on the top of an isolated hill about 2000 feet above the station. At sunset the view is wonderfully beautiful. Tradition says that the monastery was built by three kings, but does not give their names; in any case the building is of considerable antiquity. Service is held in the church three times a year. The interior has been spoiled by that fiend the "restorer." From the church you look over a wide, uninhabited valley to the giant mountain, and on turning round you see the river Terek, on the banks of which are the station and village; on either hand stretch dark cavernous-looking valleys. Beyond the Terek is the home of the Ingushes, a people who frequently carry off the cattle of their more settled neighbours, and give the small garrison of Kazbek some amusement in hunting them down.

After leaving Kazbek, we see on our right the manor-house of the princely family from which the place takes its name, a family which has produced, and doubtless will yet produce, sons which will be an honour to Georgia; the house is a fine two-storey edifice, and there is a pretty chapel attached to it. In a few minutes we reach the Mad Ravine, so called from a torrent of terrible impetuosity, which has formed one of the most serious obstacles to the construction of the road. We now enter Dariel, the pass from which the road takes its name, one of the grandest spots on earth.

According to philologists, Dariel is derived from an old Persian word meaning gate (cf. Der-bend, Thuer, door, Slav Dver, &c.), and in fact it was here that the ancient geographers placed the site of the famous Caucasian Gates; but surely there is something to be said in favour of the local tradition which connects the place with Darius I. of Persia. As for the gates, it is, of course, impossible to say definitely whether they ever existed or not, at all events there are several points where it would not have been very difficult to construct them.

At the entrance of the ravine, on the left bank of the Terek, stands a high rock, on which may be seen the ruins of a castle, said to have been founded in 150 B.C., but doubtless having a still longer history. This castle is always associated with the name of a certain wicked Queen Tamara, a mythical creation of the popular fancy, and Lermontov has written a very pretty poem based on the legend. It is said that this Tamara (not to be confounded with the good Tamara), was very beautiful, and that she used to invite all the

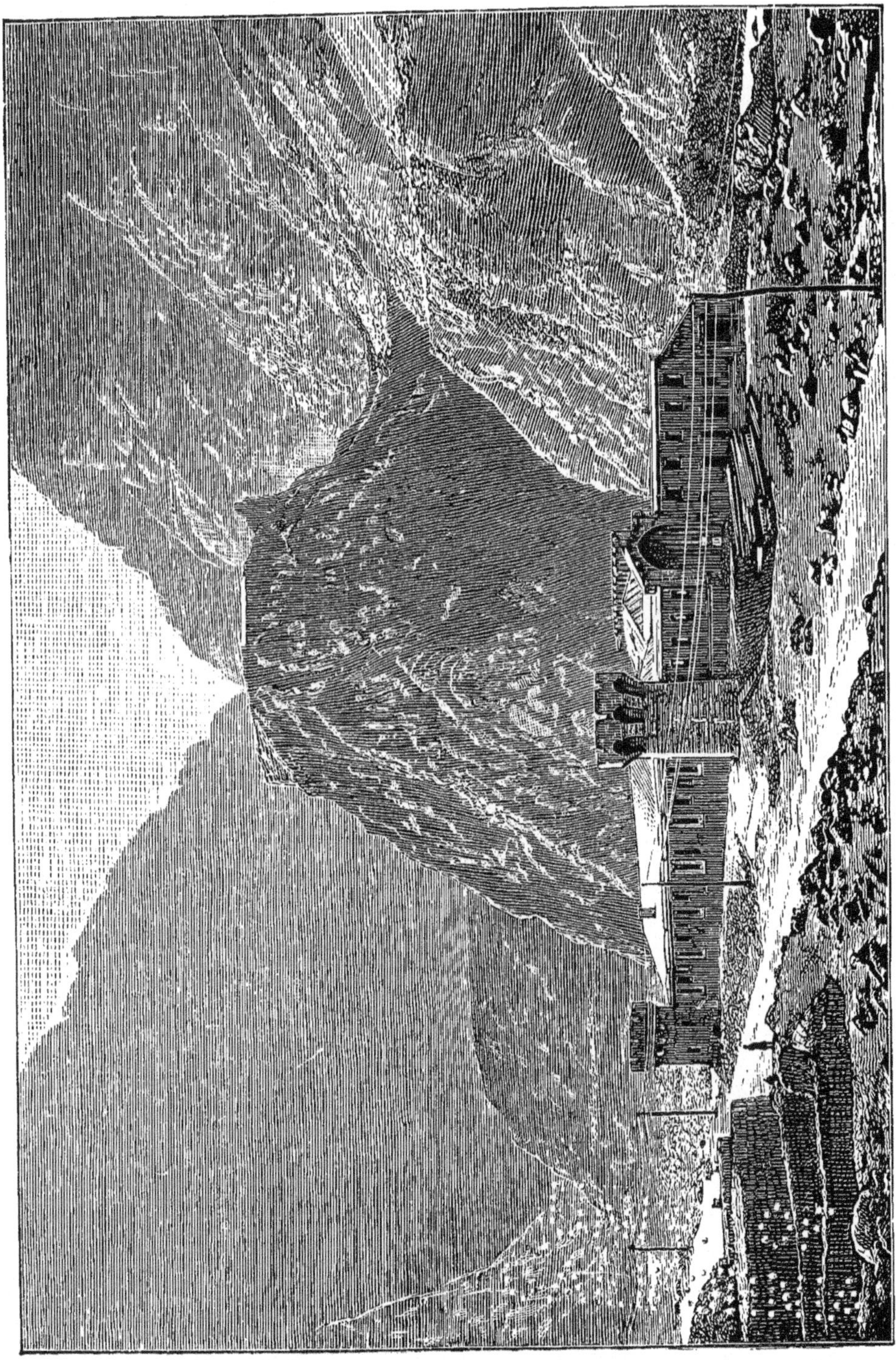

UNIV. OF
CALIFORNIA

handsome young men who passed that way to come up and live with her, promising them all the delights that heart could wish for; after one night of bliss the unfortunate gentleman was deprived of his head, and was then thrown down into the Terek, which bore away his body. If the legend is not wrong in saying that the river carried away the corpses, the frolicsome monarch must have been comparatively constant during the summer months, or else the pile of wantons would soon have become large enough to frighten all the passion out of intending visitors, for in the month of June, Terek would not float a respectably-sized cat.

By the road-side is Dariel Fort, a romantic-looking place with old-fashioned battlemented towers; a few Kazaks are quartered here, and must find the time hang very heavily on their hands. When you reach this fort it looks as if it were impossible to go beyond it, a mighty wall stretches right across the path; but the road follows the course of the river, indeed it is built in the river-bed, and winds along between awful cliffs whose summits are lost in the clouds, and whose flanks are seldom or never touched by a ray of sunlight. We sometimes hear of places where a handful of men could keep back an army, this is one of them; a touch would send down upon the road some of the heavy, overhanging masses of rock, and effectually close the pass. About fifty years ago an avalanche fell here, from the glacier of Devdorak, and it was two years before the rubbish was all cleared away. When the new road is blocked by snow or carried away by floods, the old road, high up near the snow-line, has to be used.

The scenery of this pass has been described by Pushkin, Lermontov, and many others, but it is one of the few places that do not disappoint the traveller, however much he may have expected. It must not be forgotten that the road through this narrow gorge is the only passable one that crosses the Caucasian range; there are, it is true, one or two other tracks, but they are not practicable for wheeled carriages.

In the most gloomy part of the defile the road crosses by a bridge to the left bank of the Terek, and a few versts farther on we emerge into comparatively open ground at *Lars*. I had, as usual, given my *podorozhnaia* (road-pass) to a stable-boy, with a request to get the horses ready without delay, and was sitting drinking tea, when I was astonished to hear behind me the long unfamiliar tones of my native language; I was still more

DARIEL. Page 64.

surprised when I saw that the speaker was the *starosta*, or superintendent of the station (the Government inspector, or *smatritel*, is the real chief). He told me that he had seen from my pass that I was English, and had taken the liberty to come and have a chat with me. He spoke English fluently, and has spent five years in London, has travelled in the United States, and is altogether a very pleasant fellow; he had only been at Lars a year and a half, and during all that time had not seen an Englishman. We parted very good friends, expecting to meet again when I returned from Vladikavkaz.

The village of Lars, north of the post-house, is inhabited, among others, by some of the Tagaur Ossets, descended from Tagaur, an individual who at a remote period was heir to the Armenian throne, and fled to the mountains for fear of his younger brothers. Their royal descent leads them to think themselves superior to the poor folk among whom they dwell, and they are cordially disliked by the latter. Just outside the village is one of the towers which are so common all along the road; it doubtless yielded a handsome revenue to its owner in the good old days when every traveller had to pay a heavy toll for the privilege of passing one of these fortresses.

We still keep close to the Terek, which comes rushing down from Dariel with a fall of one foot in every thirty. Pushkin, comparing the Terek with Imatra, in Finland, unhesitatingly declares the superiority of the former in grandeur. Of course the surrounding scenery in the two cases is quite different, but as far as the rivers themselves are concerned, I must dissent from the poet, for I know no part of the Terek worthy of comparison with the fall of the Wuokses at Imatra, which is the very materialization of the idea of irresistible, pitiless power.

Although the valley is now a little wider than it was a few miles to the south, the scenery still has the same grandeur and sternness until we pass between the rocks that come down close to either bank of the river, and come out into the plain in which stands Fort Djerakhovsk, a rectangular edifice, about 120 feet long, which is fully garrisoned. We are not quite clear of the mountains, however, until we have passed *Balta*, and have got within five versts of Vladikavkaz. Before us stretches a smooth, green plain as far as the eye can reach; the contrast is most striking; it is as if we had been suddenly transported from Switzerland to Holland.

Vladikavkaz, 200 versts from Tiflis, lies at the

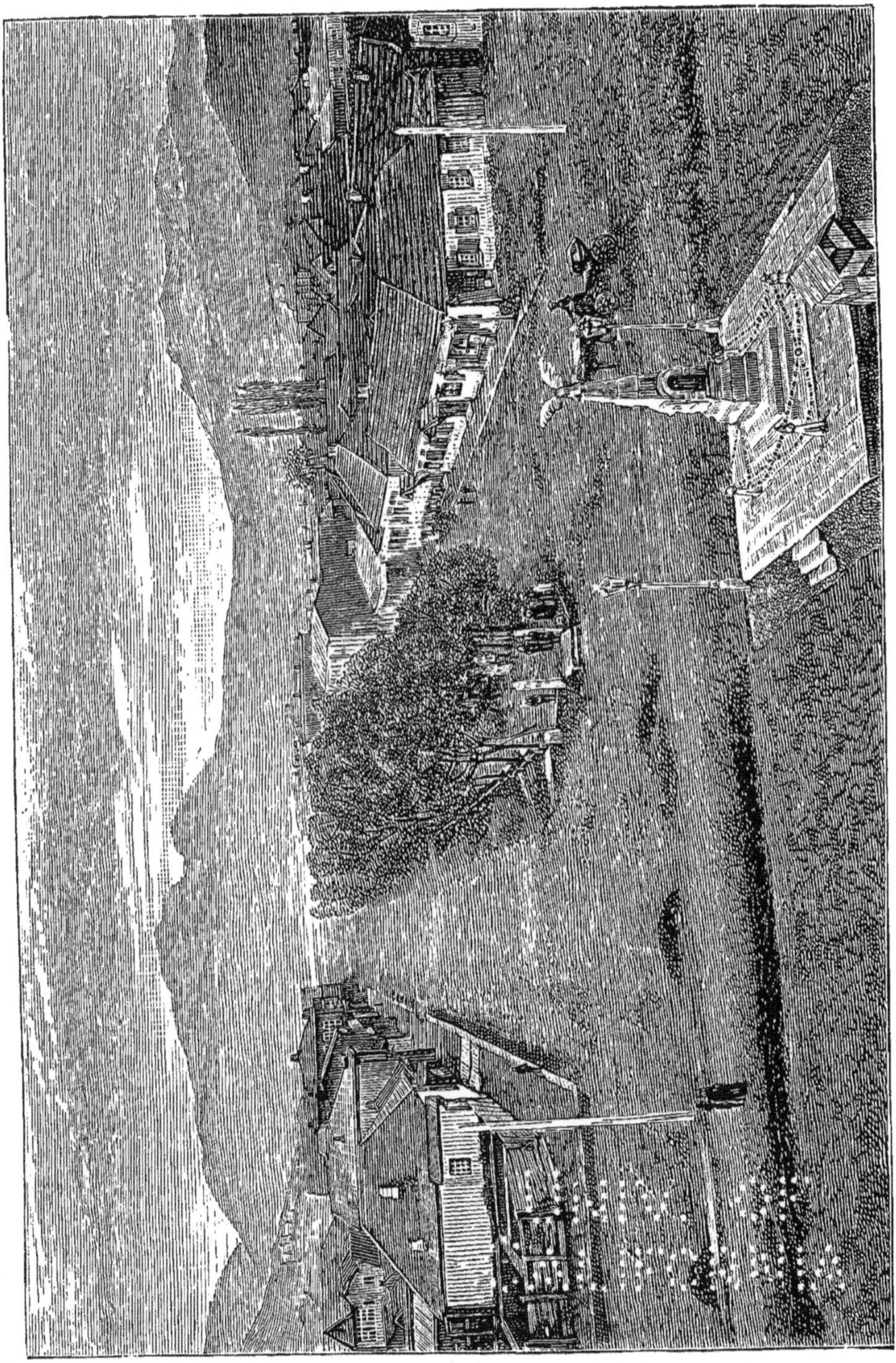

Library of
California

foot of the Caucasus, at a height of 2368 feet. The best hotel is the Pochtovaya, at the post-station; the Frantsiya is also good. Vladikavkaz means, in Russian, "master of the Caucasus" (cf. Vladivostok, Vladimir, &c.—root *vlad* is akin to German *walt*-en, Ge*walt*); the Cherkesses (Circassians) call it Kapkai, "gate of the mountains." It has a population of over 30,000 souls, chiefly Russians, Cherkesses, Georgians, Armenians, Persians, besides a strong garrison. A fortress was built here in 1784, but the town never became a trading centre of much importance until the war with Shamil; even now one is astonished to see how little activity there is in a place through which nearly all the overland traffic between Europe and Western Asia passes. Several chimney stalks bear witness to the existence of industry, but the only manufactory of any size is a spirit distillery. The silver work of Vladikavkaz is renowned throughout the whole Caucasus, and is much used for dagger hilts and sheaths, belts, &c.

The city is built on the banks of the Terek, which is here crossed by several bridges; the best quarter is on the right bank, where there are cool, shady gardens by the waterside, and a very respectable-looking boulevard. A few of the streets are fairly well paved, and there are one or two comfortable-looking houses with pleasant grounds; but on the whole the place is not one that anybody would care to settle down in. Were it not for the frequency with which one sees Asiatic costumes, and hears Asiatic tongues, and the fact that the frosty Caucasus may be seen, apparently perpendicular, rising to its loftiest points, it would be easy to imagine oneself in some provincial town not 100 versts from Moscow, instead of being 2000 versts from it.

When you have lounged in the gardens, and on the boulevard, visited the cathedral, which is still in course of construction, the market, the military school, and the old fortress, you have obtained all the diversion that is to be had in Vladikavkaz, unless you are fortunate enough to find the little theatre open, and the best thing to be done is to take the morning train to the Mineral Waters station (186 versts in nine hours) for the town called Five Mountains (Pyatigorsk), about twenty versts from the railway, which for almost a hundred years has enjoyed the reputation of being the most fashionable inland watering-place in the Russian Empire.

THE KAKHETIAN ROAD—TIFLIS TO SIGNAKH.

A FEW days after my return from Vladikavkaz, I made preparations for leaving Tiflis. It was near the end of June, and the unbearable heat had driven away nearly all those who were free to go; all the highways leading out of the city were crowded with carts and carriages of every description, carrying household goods and passengers. My friends had contracted with some Molokans (Russian heretics), belonging to the colony of Azamburi, for the removal of their furniture to Signakh; the carriers had promised to come to our house at four o'clock in the morning, but it was nine o'clock before they put in an appearance, and then their carts were half full of other people's goods, a direct violation of the agreement. If any man ever needed the patience which is proverbially ascribed to the patriarch Job, it is the man who has business dealings with the Muscovite *muzhik*. You may assail him with all the abuse which your knowledge of his language will permit, you may strike him, you may calmly endeavour to persuade him with the most lucid logic—it is all to no purpose; taking off his cap to scratch his head, he looks at you with an assumption of childlike simplicity, and replies with a proverb more remarkable for its laconism than for its applicability to the matter under discussion. In this case we wrangled for a long time, and then, being unwilling to risk a stroke of apoplexy by getting into a rage, appealed to the majesty of the law, represented by a stalwart policeman, at whose command the carts were emptied forthwith, the contents being deposited on the roadside, and our effects were soon put in their place, and the whole caravan rattled down the hillside about two hours before noon. An hour later a four-horse carriage with springs arrived, and the four of us, my Georgian host, a Russian lady and gentleman, and myself, set out for Kakheti.

After descending through the narrow streets which lie between the Erivan square and the river, we crossed the busy bridge, and mounted the steep bank on the other side, passing through the liveliest part of the Persian quarter. By the time we had got clear of the suburb called the Dogs' Village, with its camels and caravanserais, we had overtaken the waggons; exchanging friendly salutations with our volunteer baggage-guard, we were soon rolling along the smooth, dusty road in the direction of Orkhevi. On our right, down by the side of the Kura, lay Naftluk, with its beautiful vineyards and orchards, and beyond it the road to Akstafa and Erivan; on the distant southern horizon were the blue mountains of Armenia. On our left hand rose a range of bare-looking hills of no great height.

The region through which the Kakhetian road passes is a flat, waterless, almost uninhabited steppe; the winds which sometimes sweep across it are so violent that it is the custom to seek shelter from them by building the houses in the ground, with the roof on a level with the road. Twenty years ago the "Society for the Re-establishment of Orthodox Christianity in the Caucasus" obtained from the late Tsar a large concession of land near Kara Yazi, and spent 370,000 roubles on the construction of a canal for irrigation (Mariinskii Kanal); the scheme was never completely carried out, and the results obtained have not hitherto been such as to encourage the society, although a few Nestorians, Assyrian Christians, have been induced to settle in this unhealthy land. There are still unmistakable signs of the fact that in ancient times all this steppe was watered from the Kura by an elaborate system of irrigation, which must have made the country very fertile; now the whole tract is an almost unbroken wilderness, where the antelope wanders, unharmed by any hunter.

At *Orkhevi* there is nothing but the station-house, and those whose only experience of posting has been derived from the military road between Tiflis and Vladikavkaz, are likely to be unpleasantly surprised at the primitive appearance of this traveller's rest. A bare, dirty room, with two wooden benches and a table, the walls tastefully decorated with official notices, among which the most prominent is one in four languages warning farmers against the phylloxera, thereon portrayed in all the various phases of its development. Such is my remembrance of Orkhevi. The only refreshment obtainable is a *samovar* (tea-urn) of boiling water, from which you can make your own tea if you have the necessary ingredients with you. A former journey along this road had already made me familiar with all the little discomforts and privations which must be undergone by the visitor to Kakheti, so I was not disappointed. None of the stations are any better all the way to Signakh, and he who does

UNIV. OF
CALIFORNIA

AN ARBA

Page 73.

not bring with him his own food for the journey is likely to have a very good appetite by the time he reaches his destination.

The sun had now reached the meridian, and beat down upon us with terrible force, for our carriage was an open one; we were half-choked with the dust, a thick white layer of which covered us from head to foot; on either side lay bare, brown fields, baked hard as stone, and deeply fissured; no water anywhere; the only thing which broke the monotony of the scene was the occasional passage of a train of *arbas*, laden with huge, bloated-looking ox-skins, full of wine. The *arba* is the national vehicle of Georgia, and is said to have been used as a chariot by the ancient kings; it is constructed entirely of wood; there is not so much as a nail or pin of metal in it; the wheels are generally made of one piece of timber, and for this reason the *arba* is allowed to travel on the highways without paying the tolls which are imposed on carts with tires; a pair of oxen draw the cart, and the creaking of it may be heard afar off. Parched with thirst, and almost stifled with dust, we were glad to reach *Vaziani*, where we spread our cloaks under an oak-tree by the side of a spring, and proceeded to make a good lunch, after which we slept for a while.

In the afternoon we left Vaziani, and soon passed through the prosperous German colony of Marienfeld, with its neat, homely cottages, shaded by fine poplar-trees. The vicinity of the river Iora makes this a very fertile spot, cool and inviting even in the middle of summer. A little before reaching Marienfeld we saw, on the left, the road to Telav, and the Kakhetian hills now seem to slope down very quickly to meet our road, but we know that we shall have to travel many a weary verst before we reach them. In the evening, at about six o'clock, we arrived at Azamburi, a Russian village not far from the station of *Sartachali* It had been agreed that we should spend the night here, so we alighted at the *postoyalii dvor*, or inn.

Azamburi is exactly like any other Russian village, a long, dirty, double row of wretched hovels. Each farmer has his house and buildings arranged round a square courtyard, in the midst of which lie carts, pigs, agricultural produce, and filth of all kinds. The inhabitants are Molokans; some account of the religious opinions of these people will be found in Mr. D. M. Wallace's well-known work on Russia; they have no priests nor sacraments, neither smoke nor drink, do not swear, and pay great reverence to the

Bible, a copy of which may be seen on a shelf in the living-room of every house. They are not at all attractive, either in physiognomy or conversation; their awful stupidity and ugliness are all the more powerfully felt from the contrast which the native population presents to them. Their choice of a piece of ground for colonization would be inexplicable did we not remember their peculiar religious convictions; they have chosen the very worst place in the whole plain; the only drinking water in the neighbourhood is very bad, so bad that the tea made from it is almost undrinkable, even by people accustomed to Kura water. Quite near the village are stinking, stagnant marshes, which must make the place terribly unhealthy

After dinner we went outside to smoke, for the Molokan will not suffer the mildest cigarette in his house, and even in the depth of winter the visitor who smokes must burn his weed in the open air. Returning along the road for some little distance, followed by a crowd of children, who, evidently, had never before seen a lady in European dress, we mounted a little hill, whence we saw in the distance our baggage-waggons slowly approaching. In re-entering the village we overtook a farmer with an English reaping-machine; this man was less taciturn than his neighbours, and of his own accord entered into conversation with us; he was loud in his praises of the reaper, and said that the man who invented a certain part of it (a patent screw, I think) ought to be "kissed behind the ear." We tried to interest him in a pet idea of our own, viz., that village communities should buy machinery collectively, but we regret to say that we could not make a convert of him.

It was nine o'clock before our young friend, Prince Giorgi, arrived with the goods under his charge; and while we were at supper much merriment was caused by his vain endeavours to check himself in the use of the word *chort* (the devil!), a pet expression of his, but strictly forbidden in the houses of all good Molokans. The night being fine, although the air was cool, we made up our minds to sleep outside rather than risk the onslaughts of the Molokan fleas, and we chose for our bivouac a thrashing-floor about a hundred yards from the house; here we lay down, wrapped in our *burkas*, and smoked and chatted until we fell asleep. But we were not to have a quiet night; we were roused by the attack of some ferocious dogs; we beat them off several times, but the numbers ever increased, until all the canine population of Azamburi was howling round us.

We were on foot at three o'clock, and, waking

up the drivers, got the horses harnessed and started for Kakabeti. In the early morning air flitted beautiful birds with wings as brilliant as those of butterflies, and butterflies as big as birds. It was not so terribly hot as I had found it some weeks before, when I passed through Kakabeti in the afternoon, but it was still close enough to make us long for a breath of the mountain air This region is swampy, and the fevers make it uninhabitable.

Kakabeti offers nothing of interest. The same wearisome plain stretches all the way to *Kajereti*, near which is the hospitable abode of one of the Andronikov family. We spent four hours there, and did not leave the station until an hour after noon. Passing the inviting-looking post-road to Bakurtsikhe, on our left, we kept to the plain for a while; then rapidly rising to the village of Nukriani, Signakh came into view at the top of the hill, and the lovely woodlands at our feet seemed all the more beautiful on account of the bare, monotonous character of the parched plain where we had spent the last two days. Descending by a zigzag road, we entered the town, and, passing along the main street, through the market-place, soon reached the very edge of the steep, high hill which rises from the Alazana valley.

SIGNAKH.

Our new home turned out to be a very delightful place,—large, lofty rooms, two balconies; at the back, vineyards and gardens stretching far down the hillside. The view was more beautiful than any I had ever seen or imagined. The house was built on the edge of a deep, narrow ravine, the steep sides of which were covered with vines and mulberry-trees all the way down to the Alazana valley, a smooth, fertile plain thirty miles broad. On the opposite side of the ravine, to the left, stood a very extensive fortification with ruined towers, a stronghold of some importance during the war with Shamil; behind this could be seen the Armenian church and the outskirts of the town. Straight in front lay the grand Caucasian mountains, rising like a wall from the plain, their glittering snow-clad tops dividing the dark forests on their flanks from the deep blue of the summer sky. In the midst of the plain flowed the silvery Alazana, in its winding course dividing the cultivated land on this side from the virgin forest beyond. Along the nearer edge lay scattered hamlets with their neat little white churches; farther off might be seen a wood, which we always thought of as that of the Sleeping Beauty. From the heights of Signakh it does not look large, but it is six miles in diameter, and the underwood is so thick that it can only be penetrated by cutting a path with axes; it is full of all sorts of wild beasts and dangerous reptiles. In the distance on the left may be seen the mountains on which Telav is situated; to the extreme right a few huts on the river bank indicate the position of the Alazana bridge, and beyond this begins the long sandy steppe which stretches in unbroken barrenness to the Caspian.

Signakh is 100 versts to the eastward of Tiflis, and stands about 1000 feet above the plain of the Alazana. The population is over 10,000, the majority being Armenian shop-keepers, usurers, &c. The name signifies "city of refuge," and the place was founded and fortified in the last century, in order to serve as a retreat for the country people in times of Lesghian raids. The fortress consists of a very large piece of ground enclosed by high walls, with towers at regular intervals, and the whole city used to be within these walls. The post-road to Bakurtsikhe runs through the stronghold, and about sunset all the wealth and beauty of Signakh may be seen promenading on the highway, for this is "the boulevard;" on Sunday afternoon wrestling goes on merrily to the sound of the pipe and drum. At present the military importance of Signakh is almost at an end, but if Russia should ever find herself involved in a great war we might probably hear something of the doings of the Lesghians in that region. The garrison is very small.

The Club is the centre of all the social life of Signakh, and on Saturday evenings there are informal dances, to which the stranger looks forward as a welcome break in the monotony of provincial life. The Gostinnitsa "Nadezhda" (Hope Inn), which we nicknamed "Grand Hôtel de Kakhétie," is dirty and uninviting to a degree which Europeans could hardly imagine possible · but it is the best hostelry in the town. The Court-house is just opposite the inn, and I remember spending a very interesting evening there on one occasion, watching the trial of Georgians, Tatars, Armenians, by a Russian justice of the peace in a gorgeous uniform. The cases were settled with a rapidity to which the High Court of Chancery is a stranger.

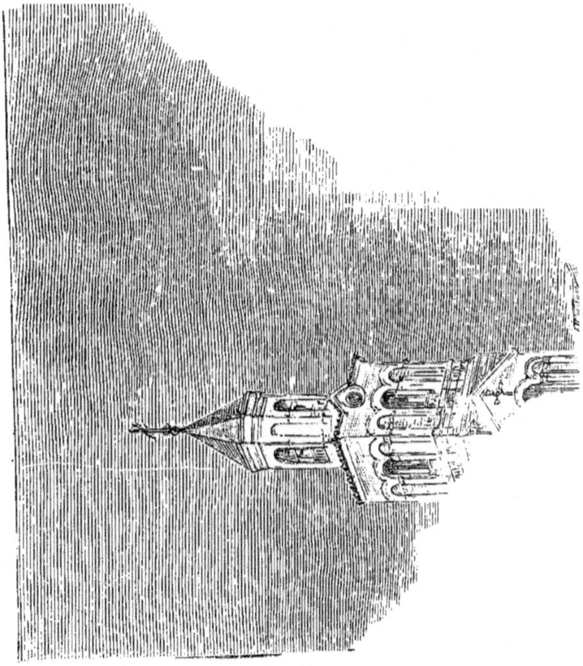

UNIV. OF
CALIFORNIA

Altogether, Signakh is a dirty but highly picturesque little town; its streets are narrow, crooked, and ill-paved, the shops, as is usual in the East, are small, open rooms, in which saddlers, tailors, and smiths may be seen plying their respective trades; all round about the town are beautiful hills covered with oak, walnut, and other tall forest-trees. The only other place it reminded me of was Amalfi, and even in this case the resemblance was but slight.

On one of the neighbouring hills, at Bodbé, is the Monastery of St. Nina. This venerable relic stands in one of the finest pieces of scenery in all Kakheti, and is surrounded by a thick forest, which has from the earliest times been protected from destruction by a popular tradition, declaring that he who breaks off a branch therein will die within the same year. The monastery was originally built by King Mirian immediately after the death of the apostle of Georgia, and her tomb may still be seen in the present church, which, according to an inscription on one of the walls, was restored by a certain King Giorgi, after the country had been laid waste by Tamerlan. In the sacristy are many old manuscripts, amongst which there are doubtless some of great historical interest, but, as far as I know, they have not yet been catalogued. On the occasion of my visit to Bodbé I passed a wine-shop, where three or four Georgians were making merry; they pressed me to stay and drink with them, but, offering them my thanks, I begged to be excused on the ground of want of time. On my return they came out, hat in hand, to the middle of the road, and presented me with a goblet, which I could not refuse to drain without giving serious displeasure to my kind entertainers. This little incident is a very good illustration of the Georgian character: when the Georgian is merry, everybody else must share his jollity or he is unhappy. I have seen a squire quite unnecessarily leave a scene of revelry for a minute or two in order to heap up food in his horse's manger, so that the faithful beast might share in the universal joy.

A TRIP ACROSS THE ALAZANA.

BAKURTSIKHE—KARTUBAN—LAGODEKH.

By daily excursions among the sloping vine-clad hills I soon made myself familiar with Kakheti, the garden of Georgia; at Kodalo I had shared the munificent hospitality of the Andronikovs, at Bakurtsikhe that of the Vachnadzes; but I had never been in the wild country beyond the Alazana, and it was with pleasure that I accepted the invitation of the Princes Vachnadze to accompany them on their yearly visit to their estates at Kartuban, on the River Kabalo, at the foot of the mountains on the other side of the plain.

Accordingly, on a certain bright summer morning our cavalcade might have been seen winding down the steep main street of Signakh. The first halting-place was to be Bakurtsikhe, seventeen versts from Signakh, where we had been invited to meet a large company of Kakhetian squires and ladies at dinner. Our path, for some miles after leaving the town, lay in the dry bed of a torrent. The remembrance of the wild, beautiful scenery of that narrow gorge still fills me with delightful emotions. It was the scene of so many pleasant rides—in the fierce heat of the noonday sun, in the cool of evening, after midnight on stormy nights, when we had returned homewards drenched with rain, our path illumined only by dazzling flashes of lightning. As we picked our way among the stones we met many a courteous gentleman, most of them clad in the same Circassian garb as ourselves, but not a few, especially the older men, in the true national garb—a short tunic, with long flaps of cloth hanging from the shoulders; a dress said to resemble the ancient Polish costume. Each raised his tall *papakh* of Astrakhan fur, and, with graceful bow, saluted us, after the manner of the country, with the word *Gamardjwéba*, which is, being interpreted, "I wish thee the victory," to which we answered *Gaguimardjos*—"May God grant thee the victory." These salutations are as eloquent as a dozen volumes of history. I never heard them without thinking of the sad but glorious past of the Georgian kingdom, nobly holding its own, unaided, and witnessing for Christ and His Cross against all the hosts of Islam, performing prodigies of valour that would

GEORGIAN NATIONAL COSTUME.
Page 84.

AUSTRALIA

have added to the fame of Greece or Rome. God grant thee the victory, brave Georgia!

Emerging from the glen, we joined the post road at Anaga, and our impatient horses set off at a gallop. On we sped through the well-kept vineyards of a Russian capitalist, Count Sheremetiev, who threatens to ruin all the poor squires of the district by selling his wines under cost price. At a little village, about half-way between Signakh and Bakurtsikhe, two of us had far outstripped the rest, and were racing neck to neck when my companion's horse cast a shoe; so leaving him at a roadside smithy, I went on alone. The fierce summer sun stood high in the blue arch of heaven; on my left were vine-clad crags; to the right, beyond the river, rose the white peaks of the mountain wall between me and Europe. But I thought not of Europe. I forgot kindred, country, humanity—everything. My horse and I were one, and we were merged in that great, living ocean of life—our mother earth. My pulse beat in harmony with the heart of Nature herself, keeping time with the rippling rills, the whisper of the wandering airs to the leaves of the trembling trees. I had entered a blissful Nirvana, in which all consciousness of self was swallowed up in the world's soul.

I had ridden half a mile beyond the point whence I should have ascended by a bridle-path to our host's house, before the cool shade of a cliff aroused me from my state of forgetfulness. It was on the summit of this cliff that my friends had recently met their tenants to discuss some little differences that had arisen between them. Honest folk do not like law-courts—especially Russian law-courts—so the good Kakhetians decided to settle their dispute in the old-fashioned, orthodox manner. A couple of horses were killed, and a good many men on either side were pretty severely hacked and bruised; but the landlords came off victorious. They, nevertheless, agreed to grant certain concessions to the farmers, so all left the field of battle delighted with one another. It is only just to say that this case was an exceptional one. The relations between the gentry and peasantry are excellent; they are on terms of such affectionate familiarity that the latter always address their prince by his pet name.

Soon after noon we were all enjoying the hospitality of our friend. When I say hospitality, I am not using the word in its conventional sense; a Georgian displays towards his guest such courtesy and kindness as are unknown among

European peoples. Other friends soon arrived, and at three o'clock, the usual dinner-hour, a score of us sat down to dine in a shady arbour on the hillside. The dishes were purely Oriental; rich *pilavi* (rice cooked with fruits, pistachio nuts, &c.), *shishlik* (a choice cut of mutton roasted on a silver skewer over a yard long, on which it is served up), and many another delicacy, the thought of which makes my mouth water even now. The wine deserves special mention. Kakheti has one of the finest soils in the world for grape-growing, and any kind of wine, including fine champagne, can be produced there. Unfortunately, the people in general have not yet become acquainted with the methods by which wine has to be "manipulated" in order to make it at once agreeable to a European palate. Some of the best brands are not, however, open to this objection, and are largely sold in Petersburg and Moscow, but they are not so well known as they deserve to be. Merchants discourage the introduction of new wines, as our Australian and South African fellow-subjects know to their cost; but the day will undoubtedly come when Caucasian vintages will be known and appreciated.

The drinking habits of the Georgians are interesting. A toastmaster (*tolumbash*) is always chosen, and it is his duty to propose the health of each guest in turn. To those who do not drain their glasses before the time for the next toast has arrived, the *tolumbash* cries *Alaverdi!* to which the laggard replies, *Yakhsheol*, and immediately finishes the draught, in order to escape the penalty of swallowing a large hornful of liquor at a breath. These words are of Tatar origin, and commemorate a brave Tatar named Alaverdi, who fell in a battle between the Georgians and Persians. The glasses contain a quarter of a pint, and the stranger who sits down with a score of friends is somewhat apprehensive as to the condition in which he will leave the table. Luckily, the wine is nothing but pure grape-juice, and a person with a tolerably strong head can dispose of two or three quarts of it without feeling much the worse. Each toast is accompanied by the singing of a grand old song called *Mraval djamier ghmerthma inebos* (May God grant thee many years), to which the person thus honoured must sing the reply, *Madlobeli vart* (I thank you). I have transcribed the song in the Appendix. The ladies drink water scarcely coloured with wine.

Our dinner lasted more than two hours, and concluded with some miscellaneous toasts, among which those of England and her Queen were received with the greatest enthusiasm. Then, after tea, the guests amused themselves with music and dancing, and nightfall found us all, young and old, chasing one another about on the hillside in the games of cat-and-mouse and blindman's buff. It was past midnight before we retired to rest; some of us lay on the low, carpet-covered *takhti*, or divans, which in Georgia replace beds, while those who preferred it slept out on the green, wrapped up in their cloaks.

It had been arranged that we should start for the Alazana on the following morning at four o'clock, in order to escape the terrible midday heat of the low-lying plains by the river-side; but when we rose we found that a couple of the horses had disappeared, and this delayed us for two or three hours. At length we started, and, waving farewells to all our good friends at Bakurtsikhe, we proceeded down the long slope to the plain. There were six of us, besides a servant, and we were armed to the teeth, after the manner of the country, with daggers, pistols, swords, and rifles—not an unnecessary precaution, for we saw ploughmen with a double-barrelled gun slung over the shoulder, and sword and dagger at the girdle, while a man stood at the end of the furrow ready to give the alarm. These fertile lands are only half tilled. The wild Lesghian marauders come down upon the farms, and steal all that can be carried away, and in the event of a war they would simply burn up the whole country to the very gates of Tiflis.

It was a weary journey down to the river-bank, and we did not reach the ferry until noon. The ferryman lives in a hut a good way from the river, and it was only after firing half a dozen shots in the air that we succeeded in attracting his attention. That half-hour of waiting among the reeds, with the sun right overhead, was the warmest half-hour I ever spent. At length the ferry-boat, a long tree-trunk with the inside burnt out of it, came across the stream, and we took our saddles and bridles and laid them in it. The horses had, of course, to swim, and it was a long and difficult task to get them all over. The current is very strong, and it was a subject for congratulation that none of them were carried away by it. Excepting at the ferry, the banks are so steep that it is impossible to land. When all had safely reached the other side we lay down under the shade of the trees, and lunched off cucumbers and coarse bread, washed down by the white Kakhetian wine, of which we carried a full sheepskin.

The hottest part of our day's work was over; instead of burnt, shadowless plains we should now have the sunless forest to ride through until we reached our halting-place for the night. But we well knew that we should not be in clover for the rest of the day, for we had often been told that this wood was infested by a horse-fly of a very malignant character, and as we rode along the northward path we had an opportunity of making the acquaintance of the insect in question. Within a mile of the bank we were surrounded by swarms of them, and the horses, becoming more and more restless, at last went perfectly mad with pain, while the blood dripped plentifully from their flanks. To think of holding them in by bit and bridle was out of the question, the only thing to be done was to let them gallop ahead and to keep a sharp look-out for the many boughs that overhung the scarcely perceptible track. Although Georgia is not in the tropics, this was a truly tropical forest with all its luxuriant and beautiful vegetation; walnut and other fancy woods abound, but they are allowed to fall and rot unutilized; the undergrowth on either hand is so thick as to be impenetrable; on all sides are masses of strange, bright flowers, making the air heavy with perfume, and birds of dazzling plumage sit chattering on every tree.

About an hour before sunset we reached the river Kabalo, a swift, shallow mountain stream, which we forded, and then rode up a fine glade to the encampment of my friends' Tatar herdsmen. About a score of families live there all the summer in large tents, which are not altogether devoid of comfort; in the interior may be seen carpeted divans, gold and silver ornaments are not uncommon, and the copper household utensils are thoroughly artistic in shape and beautifully engraved. We dismounted at the chief man's tent, and, lying down on the greensward, waited impatiently for dinner. The fare was abundant and good, as was to be expected in a country so rich in game and fish, and we slaked our thirst with cool *kumiss* (fermented mare's milk). The Tatars are fine, bold-looking fellows; there is in their faces a look of wild freedom that is extremely attractive to one who has spent the most of his life in cities. I believe that if I had stayed a week or two in that camp on the Kabalo, I should have been content to renounce civilized life altogether. A very houri, a gazelle of the wilderness, a sixteen-year old maiden in red tunic and wide trousers, with long dark hair in countless tiny braids and pretty little white bare feet and ankles, cast timid glances in our direction, and lovely, languorous eyes said as plainly as possible, "Fly to the desert! fly with me" . . . and many other things which the curious reader may find recorded in the works of the late Mr. Thos. Moore.

At nightfall we rode away, accompanied by a few Tatars, to visit the large herds of horses and cattle which feed near here, and then proceeded to the little cluster of cottages where the Georgian farm-labourers live, about a couple of miles higher up the river. We were received by the steward, a Greek from Cilicia, and after chatting merrily over our tea for a few hours, we spread our *burkas* on the ground and slept as well as the clouds of fierce mosquitoes would allow us to do, under the starlit sky, lulled by the music of the stream.

About an hour before dawn the cold aroused us all, and after a bath in the icy waters of the Kabalo, and a hasty breakfast, we visited the farm-buildings. Tobacco is the chief commodity produced, but its cultivation is at present rather unprofitable; I saw three hundred bales of the finest leaves of last year's growth lying in the store unsold; it is quite equal to Turkish, and can be bought at a ridiculously low price, but it is not yet known in Europe, even in Russia "Batumskii tabak" has only recently been introduced, although it is far superior to that which is grown on the Don. Georgian landowners cannot afford to push the sale of their wares in Europe, but I am sure that if English firms would send out buyers they would not regret it, unless they dealt with the wily Armenian middle-man instead of the Georgian producer. The fear of the Lesghian robber-bands prevents any great outlay of capital in the development of such a district, and, indeed, nobody in Georgia has much capital to spare, so the greater part of the estate I am speaking of, hundreds of square miles in extent, is a pathless forest.

By eight o'clock we were in the saddle. The path rises through thick woodlands to the summit of a hill crossed by a narrow, rocky pass which has an unpleasant reputation as being the haunt of brigands; only a few weeks before, a party of travellers had been attacked there, two of their number were wounded, and they were all relieved of their purses, jewellery, and arms. We were within half a mile of the top when we perceived a Lesghian prowling about a little in advance of us.

We halted, unslung our fire-arms and loaded, then extending for attack, as far as the nature of of the country would allow, we went forward at a quick walking pace. We soon caught sight of three more Lesghians, but this was evidently the whole force, for they contented themselves with looking at us from a distance, and seeing that the odds were in our favour, they galloped away into the depths of the forest, and left us to pursue our journey unmolested.

Climbing to the summit of the hill, we enjoyed a splendid view of the Alazana valley from the opposite side to that whence we had been accustomed to see it; behind us rose the white peaks of the Caucasus, looking very near in the clear morning air. A little way off the blue smoke rising from among the trees showed us where our friends, the highwaymen, were cooking their breakfast. To the eastward, almost at the foot of the hill, lay the Russian military colony of Mikhailovka, to which we descended.

Mikhailovka is fairly prosperous compared with other Russian colonies in Transcaucasia, but to a European it does not seem an Arcadia; it is one wide, straggling street of poor, dirty-looking farmhouses. The colonists have to struggle with fever and ague, not to speak of Lesghians, and altogether do not seem to enjoy their life very much. Mikhailovka is the point at which the military road from Signakh turns to the eastward, and about five miles farther on arrives at Lagodekh, the staff head-quarters of an army corps, into which we rode about an hour before noon.

Lagodekh is a place of some size, with wide, clean streets and large grassy squares, planted with fine trees, the houses are neat and comfortable looking. Swift mountain streams run through it and supply delicious water. The public buildings comprise barracks, hospital, stores, a fine church of red sandstone, a modest club-house, bazar, &c. We made our way to the quarters of an officer of the 39th, whose hospitality we enjoyed until evening. In spite of the terrible heat, our host showed us everything worth seeing. The park is the great attraction, it is beautifully kept, and contains a fine long avenue of tall poplars; in the middle of it is a pavilion with the garrison ball-room, and near the entrance may be seen a small cemetery where there is a real, old-fashioned ghost, which, under the semblance of a white lady carrying a cross, affrights the local Tommy Atkins every year in the month of June. I commend this sprite to the attention of the Psychical Research Society, and I am quite willing to proceed to Lagodekh and spend a month there in investigating the matter—at the Society's expense.

The troops suffer a good deal in the summer months, and there are many casualties from apoplexy, dysentery, and other complaints.

Early in the afternoon we sat down to dinner, and did full justice to the fare. My neighbour on the right was the brother of a charming lady whom I had met in Tiflis, and it so happened that he had that very day received from her a letter in which I was spoken of, for Englishmen are rare birds in these lands. This gentleman had wandering proclivities almost as strong as my own, and he informed me that he thought of travelling overland by Merv to India, "where the English pay private soldiers as much as the Russians pay a captain." After dinner we all slept for an hour, and then, the heat having slightly diminished, we started for Mikhailovka. A bear hunt was to take place on the following day, and we were urgently pressed to stay and take part in it, but we had to be back in Signakh within the next twenty-four hours, and were therefore obliged to deny ourselves this pleasure.

Before we were clear of Lagodekh somebody had the unfortunate idea of starting a wild gallop, but the spot was badly chosen, for a sudden turn in the road brought us to a river with a wide, stony bed. The leading horse threw his rider into the very middle of the stream, I was deposited on a heap of big stones on the other side; all the rest, warned by our mishap, escaped. It took over an hour to catch the runaway horses, and when we reached Mikhailovka I felt as if I had passed through a thrashing-mill, every bone was aching. Our camping-ground was under a large oak-tree, behind a peasant's house, and we lay there on the ground, a prey to the mosquitoes, until early morning.

At half-past four we were in the saddle, and after a stirrup-cup of Russian vodka, galloped down the smooth, well-kept military road towards the Alazana, occasionally glancing back at the beautiful hill country behind us. I felt all my many bruises with double force after the night's rest, and it was as much as I could do to keep my seat, not to speak of emulating the exploits of my companions, who were amusing themselves with shots at the hares and feathered game with which the country abounds. At length, at about eight o'clock, we reached the *Chiauri Bridge*, a shaky-looking wooden structure. There is a wretched little wine-shop, where we dismounted for breakfast. A fine fish of fifteen pounds' weight, with some of the coarse, indiarubber-like bread of the country, formed the solid part of the meal; I need not say what the liquid part of it was; we emptied our sheepskin and then fell back on mine host's supplies. The river, in summer at least, is sluggish and dirty, and has an evil smell of decaying vegetable matter, very suggestive of malarial fever; if our acquaintance with the Alazana had been confined to this portion of it, we should have been at a loss to understand the high praise which has been bestowed on it by all the sweet singers of Rustaveli's land.

We spent a couple of hours in rest and refreshment, and then started for home across the broad plain yellow with ripe grain. Noon saw us begin the toilsome ascent of the hills of Signakh, and an hour later we were lying on our balcony dreamily smoking cigarettes of Kartuban tobacco, while we mentally retraced every step of our delightful journey among the fair scenes which now lay spread at our feet.

SIGNAKH TO TELAV, AND THENCE TO TIFLIS.

My stay in Kakheti was so pleasant that I found it very hard to leave. My good friends there insisted that I should marry a Georgian lady and settle down as a country squire, to grow wine and drink it among them for the remainder of my natural life; when I finally decided upon the day for my departure they pressed me to stay, at least, until the vintage-time, but I still had much ground to go over, and I had made up my mind to return to England before winter set in.

One morning in July I said good-bye to Signakh, and set out in a post-cart for Telav. As far as Bakurtsikhe the road was quite familiar to me; it had never seemed so beautiful as it did when I said farewell to it. Then came Kalaki, which like Bakurtsikhe, is full of members of the Vachnadze family, and Gurdjani, one of the villages belonging to the Andronikovs. The Andronikovs are descended from a Byzantine prince who fled to Georgia during the reign of Queen Tamara; they have always been distinguished for bravery and munificence, the two virtues which are most appreciated in this country; in the present century they have produced a general worthy to rank with any who have ever served the Tsars. I may say, in passing, that it is astonishing to find what a large percentage of the great military leaders in the Russian army have been and are of Georgian birth. Another curious circumstance is that some of the best families in Georgia are of foreign origin; the Bagrats, the royal family, were once Hebrews, and claim to be descended from David. the son of Jesse; the Orbelianis, the second family in the kingdom, came from China; the Andronikovs, as we have just remarked, were originally Greeks.

Near Gurdjani is *Akhtala*, a muddy hollow in which are slime baths, resorted to by persons suffering from rheumatism, scrofula, and many other diseases; the baths are simply round holes full of mud, in the middle of which an evil-smelling gas slowly bubbles up; the largest bath of all is reserved for cattle. I need hardly say that all the bathing goes on *al fresco*, for nobody has thought of building a hydropathic establishment in this remote corner of the Caucasus. Akhtala has, of course, its legend. It is said that a farmer was once working in his vineyard on the Feast of the Transfiguration, when a passer-by asked him why he was not at church on so holy a day. The scoffer replied that he had seen enough of transfigurations, he and his wife had been transfigured into old people, and their children into men and women; the wayfarer, who was none other than our Lord, said, "Well, you shall see yet another transfiguration," whereupon the ground opened, and belched forth a liquid mass, which swallowed up the vineyard, with the sinner and all his household.

The road continues to run parallel to the Alazana, and the next station is *Mukuzani*, seventeen versts from Bakurtsikhe, near which is the flourishing town of Velistsikhe. All this region is a fertile, well-cultivated plain, and there are many villages renowned for their wines; the peasants of the Telav district are much wealthier than those near Signakh. *Akuri*, fourteen versts from Mukuzani, is the last station. The city of Telav is now visible on the top of a hill straight in front, and it has a very picturesque appearance.

About half a dozen miles beyond Akuri, in a beautiful valley, is *Tsinondal*, formerly the home of Prince David Chavchavadze, but now the property of Alexander Alexandrovich, Autocrat of all the Russias, for whom a vast palace was being built at the time of my visit. The Tsar would be far safer here than at Gachina, for there are no anarchists among the Georgians, and I cannot account for the rumour that it was proposed to exile a large number of the young nobles, in order to assure the monarch's safety during his sojourn in the Caucasus.

Tsinondal is famous as the scene of one of the most dramatic incidents of the war with Shamil, viz., the capture of Princesses Chavchavadze and Orbeliani in July, 1854. On account of rumours of Lesghian raids the Chavchavadze family had not left Tiflis for their estates until the month of July. They arrived safely at Tsinondal, and were soon joined by Nina Chavchavadze's sister, Princess Varvara Orbeliani, whose husband had just been killed while fighting against the Turks. They were but newly settled in their summer quarters, when Prince Chavchavadze received orders to go and take the command of a fortress some distance from home. Before leaving, he reassured his family by telling them that reinforcements were about to be sent to Telav, and that the Alazana was so high that the enemy could not cross it. In a few days the prince wrote to his wife to say that he was besieged by a force of five or six thousand Lesghians, but had no fear of the place being taken; if he thought it advisable for his family to leave Tsinondal, he would let them know.

Meanwhile the Lesghians were nearer than was imagined, and the flames from burning villages in the neighbourhood soon warned the family that no time was to be lost. First of all the peasants came and begged the princess to fly to the woods with them; then the gentry of the district offered their aid for the same purpose, but these offers were declined; her husband had told her to stay there, and there she would stay. At length, the advance of the enemy had proceeded so far in the direction of Tsinondal, that the princess consented to have all her plate and jewels packed up one night, ready for flight on the morrow; but it was too late. Soon after dawn the Lesghians were in the gardens of the castle. The family doctor and a handful of servants gallantly held the gate for a few minutes, but they were soon shot down, and the place was in the hands of the wild men of the mountains.

The women and children sought refuge in a garret, whence they heard the smashing of mirrors, pianos, and other furniture. A few Lesghians soon discovered the hiding-place of the terrified family, and each seized a woman or child as his share of the booty. As they bore away their prisoners the staircase broke under their weight, and all fell in a confused heap on the lower floor. Then there was a murderous fight for the possession of the ladies; their garments were torn to shreds, and some of them were wounded. The conquerors picked up the senseless victims from a heap of dead Lesghians, and forced them to mount on horseback behind them.

The passage of the Alazana was accomplished with great danger, and when they reached the other side the half-naked ladies were wet, chilled, and miserable. Strange to tell, Princess Baratov, a beautiful girl of eighteen, had not lost any article of dress, and was as richly attired as if she had been on her way to a ball. But poor Mdme. Drançay, the French governess, had nothing left but a chemise and a corset. A handful of Georgians attempted a rescue; the Lesghians mistook them for the skirmishers in advance of an army, and fled. Princess Nina Chavchavadze had an infant in her arms, and after riding for some distance she was so wearied that the baby fell and was trampled under the horses' feet. She would have leaped after it, but her captor held her fast, and another man coolly cut the child's throat.

Finding the number of prisoners too large, the Lesghians killed sixty of them on the road. All the villages on the way were burned, and their inhabitants butchered. Then they mounted through a thick forest and up among the mountains to Pokhalski, where Shamil was staying with an army of ten thousand men. There they were joined by a new prisoner, Niko Chavchavadze, who, with thirty Georgians, had held a castle for three days against five hundred Lesghians, and only surrendered when he had not a cartridge left. Shamil ordered the princess to write to Tiflis saying that all the prisoners would be handed over to Russia in exchange for his son, Djemal Eddin, and a fair ransom. In the meantime the ladies had to make themselves veils of muslin, and they lived in the harem of Shamil. They were, however, treated honourably, and they always had the highest respect for the great warrior and prophet.

Eight months elapsed before the negotiations were concluded, and on the 10th of March, 1855, the exchange took place at Kasafiurte. Djemal Eddin, Shamil's son, had since his early youth been held as a hostage at Petersburg. He was a most amiable man; had become perfectly Russian in his way of life, and spoke Russian, French, and German fluently; he was colonel of a regiment, and aide-de-camp to the Tsar. It was with deep regret that he left civilization to return to the wild life of his native mountains, and in 1858 he died of a broken heart.

Mounting the sloping Tsivi hills, the road enters *Telav* by the Boulevard, at one end of which is the inn; but on my applying for lodgings I was told that the house was under repair, and travellers could not be entertained. I was recommended to go to " The Club." At the Club the room offered me was so dirty and cheerless that I decided to make the post-house my headquarters. It was only one o'clock in the afternoon, and I determined to have an early dinner. In a town like Telav, thought I, it will be possible to get something to eat. I first addressed myself to the postmaster, who replied that boiling-water was the only refreshment he could offer me, but held out the hope that I might get dinner in the town. I wandered up and down the streets for an hour, hungry, thirsty, and hot, and then found a dirty eating-house where I refreshed myself with vodka, eggs, wine, and bread. It took three quarters of an hour to boil the eggs! I leave the reader to imagine whether my first impressions of Telav were favourable or not. I returned to the station and slept.

It was beginning to get cooler before I went to examine the objects of interest in the town. Telav, the capital of the ancient kingdom of Kakheti, lies in a very strong position on two hills, about 1400 feet above the Alazana. It was founded by King Grigal I., first king of Kakheti, destroyed by the Persians under Shah Abbas in the sixteenth century, and rebuilt by Irakli II. The present population is about eight or nine thousand. In going from the post-house to the centre of the town I passed through a gateway in the old wall, which used to surround the whole city, and is of great antiquity. On the left is the palace of Irakli II., now used as a grammar-school for young gentlewomen, and in it may be seen the room where the old hero died, on January 11th, 1798. There are a couple of interesting old churches, containing curious pictures and ornaments of a certain artistic value. The main street is well paved, and has a long arcade under which are the chief shops. Telav is much more cheerful than Signakh, although the population is smaller, and there are comparatively few Armenians. From a low bridge across the dry

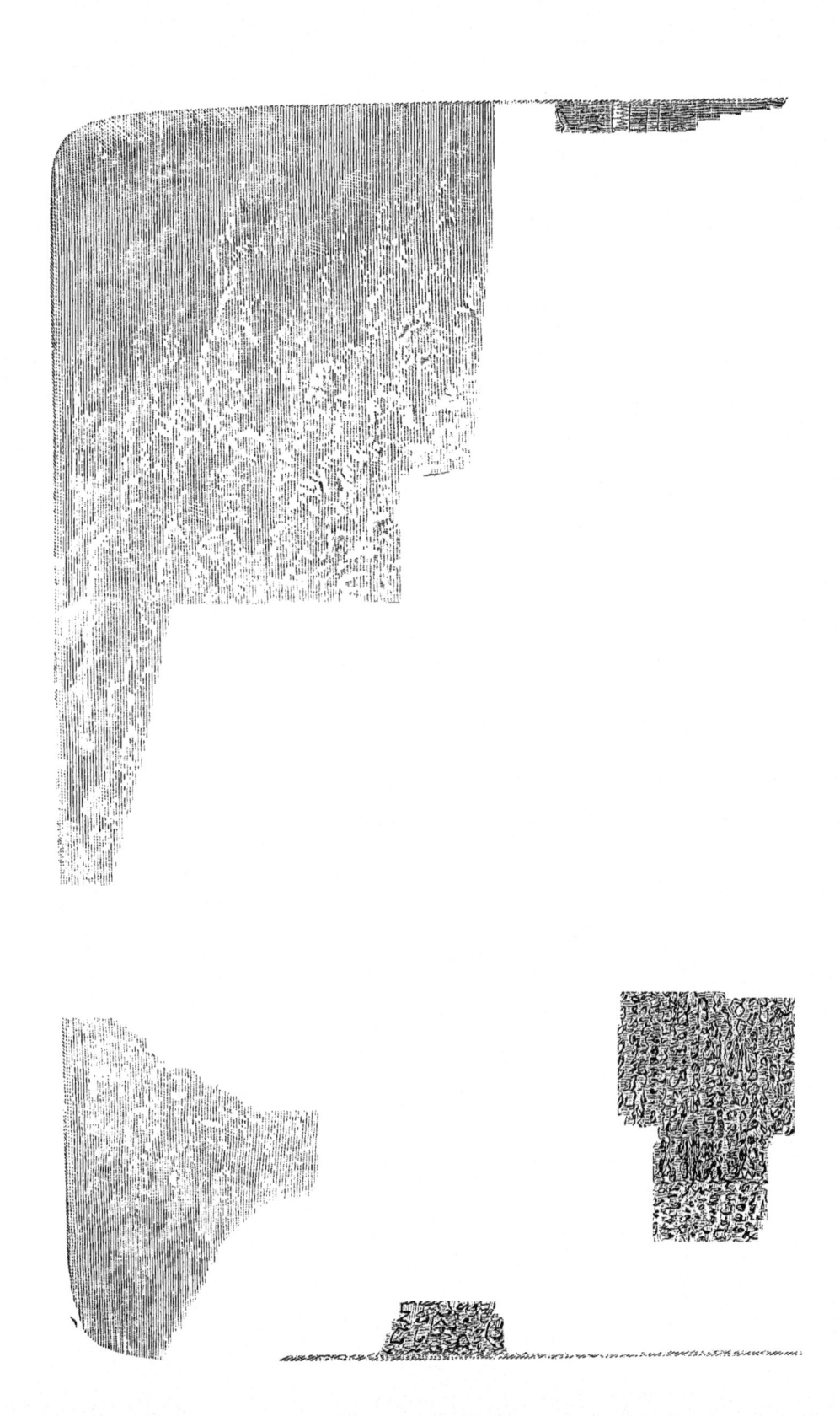

THE VISUAL
AUTOBIOGRAPHY

bed of a torrent, one gets a splendid view over the Alazana to the Caucasian range and the country of the Tushes.

When I had seen all the sights of Telav, I felt bored to death, and was just preparing to leave the Boulevard for a walk in the country, when a handsome boy of fourteen, in a cadet's uniform, ran up and welcomed me effusively. It was young Prince M——, whom I had met in Tiflis. He was soon followed by his father, a retired colonel, who has done good service for the great white Tsar, and has been wounded more than once. Although I had only seen him once or twice before, he reproached me for not coming to take up my quarters at his house, and repeatedly urged me to stay a few days with him. But I had made up my mind to leave for Tiflis early on the following morning. We took a walk in the park called Nadikari, given to the town by the Vakhvakhovs, and enjoyed enchanting views of the Alazana dale and the mountains. Returning to my friend's house, we supped, and sat over our wine until past midnight. When I left for the post-house the grey-headed warrior and his pretty son embraced me and wished me every good thing. They insisted upon sending with me a servant who carried wine and bread for my journey.

At four o'clock on the following morning I left my wooden couch, and seated myself in the stage-coach for Tiflis. I only had two companions, an Armenian trader of the most objectionable description, and a Georgian schoolmaster on his way to Odessa for a holiday. The latter was a very jolly fellow, and intelligent withal. He was an ardent champion of the doctrines of the First Revolution, and of the modern principle of nationality. He soon entered into conversation with me. My unmistakably foreign accent immediately roused his curiosity, and when I told him that I was English he steadfastly refused to believe me, asserting that I was a Mingrelian. The road passes through a few villages, and then, as it mounts by the side of the river, the houses become scarcer. On the right are many square holes in the face of a steep cliff; they are said, like those between Tiflis and Mtzkhet, to have been used as places of refuge in time of war, and they are approached from a monastery on the top of the hill. On the left is the monastery of the Mother of God, a favourite resort of the people of Telav. The track then runs along the bottom of the valley, on the right bank of the river Turdo, amid rich woodland scenery.

It takes a long time to mount to the summit of *Gambori*. This winding road had only recently been opened to traffic, and there is no posting yet. The best means of conveyance is the daily coach, and it is a slow and uncomfortable vehicle. I had been advised to make a good meal at Gambori station, and, as the coach waits there for half an hour, I entered the *dukhan*, or wine-shop, with this object in view. Alas! nothing was to be had but vodka, tobacco, and matches! Beyond Gambori the scenery becomes quite English-looking for a time. There is abundance of game of all kinds, and I saw two fine deer run across the road behind us. Climbing to a grassy knoll, bare of trees, we arrived at length at the Pass of Gambori, deservedly called Cold Mountain (6044 feet above sea level, and thirty-four versts from Telav), and, leaving Kakheti behind us, descended into the valley of the Iora and the province of Kartli. Passing the ruined castle of Verena, built in the fifth century by King Gurgaslan, we enjoy an ever-changing view of indescribable loveliness all the way to Lager.

Lager, as the name indicates, is a military post, and is of some importance on account of its position, about half-way between Tiflis and Telav; it is the summer quarters of a brigade. The garrison was not at that time very large, but there was some talk of increasing it; indeed, we met a couple of hundred men and half a dozen guns only a few versts beyond the village. The heat was terrible, and we could not help pitying the poor soldiers, who were cursing and sweating as they toiled up the mountain side. The radical schoolmaster began to descant on the advantages of universal disarmament, but he was interrupted by a good little peasant woman from the Russian colony at Lager, who replied that it was certainly very hard, but "if we had not a large army the English would come and make slaves of us all."

The next station was *Udjarma*, a fortress of great importance from the third century to the fifteenth, but now an uninteresting place, chiefly remarkable for the fact that the village graveyard is on the top of a very steep, isolated hill. From this point the road becomes dull; it crosses a bare, windy plain, and is as wearisome as the Signakh road, which it meets near Vaziani. The white church of St. David's was soon seen glittering in the sun; then Orkhevi was passed, and not long after sunset we entered Tiflis, hot, dusty, tired, and hungry, after our journey of 70 versts. I spent two days in Tiflis, where the heat had by that time become stifling; then I regretfully doffed my Circassian garb, and again submitted to the bondage of the stiff linen collar. On the afternoon of the third day I was in Baku.

THE HISTORY OF GEORGIA.

GEORGIAN history may be said to begin with *Pharnavaz*, the first king of the country, who reigned in the third century B.C. It is to him that the invention of the ordinary civil alphabet is commonly attributed. From this remote date down to the present time we have an almost unbroken narrative, the trustworthiness of which is proved by its agreement with the annals of other lands. Those who are specially interested in the early history will find in the sequel such bibliographical references as will enable them to satisfy their curiosity; but the present sketch will be confined to the more modern period, beginning in the eleventh century A.D.

In 1089 *David II.*, of the Bagratid line, descended, if we are to believe tradition, from David the Psalmist (note the harp and the sling in the royal arms of Georgia), as well as from Pharnavaz, came to the throne. During the reigns of his immediate predecessors the land had been mercilessly laid waste by the Seldjukid

Turks; but the successes of the Crusaders, and the temporary decline of the Mahometan power in the East, enabled him to raise his country to a very high position. Having boldly attacked the Turks, and driven them out of every part of his dominions, he set himself to rebuild cities, fortresses, and churches, purged the state and the church of many abuses, and liberally encouraged education. These deeds have won for him the name of *David the Renewer*. Georgia enjoyed prosperity for the next hundred years, and then came the zenith of the national glory.

In 1184 *Queen Tamara* succeeded her father, and reigned twenty-eight years, the happiest and most glorious period in the history of the country. The queen had the good fortune to be surrounded by wise counsellors and brave generals, but it is chiefly to her own virtues that her success is to be ascribed. The military exploits in which she was engaged spread her fame throughout the whole of Asia. Erzerum, Dovin, Trebizond, Sinope, Samsun, Kars, and Ani saw the triumph of the Georgian arms, the renowned Rokn Eddin was signally defeated, and the Persians were terror-stricken by her expedition to Khorassan.

Yet she did not neglect home affairs; she was the orphan's mother, the widow's judge. Religion was the moving force in everything that she did; when a large booty was captured, a portion of it was always set aside for the Blessed Virgin, and churches soon sprang up in every village. She daily spent much time in prayer, and made garments for the poor with her own fair, queenly hands. There is a tradition to the effect that she every day did as much work as would pay for her food, and although this is probably an exaggeration, it serves to show what the character of the queen was.

Her literary talents were of no mean order; when she had won a battle, she could, like Deborah, tell forth her triumph in a sweet, glad song to the Lord of Hosts, and one, at least, of these psalms is still preserved; but it is chiefly as the inspirer and patroness of poets that she is famous. Such fragments of her correspondence as we have before us reveal the fact that she was no mean diplomatist. One of them especially breathes forth a noble spirit of fearless faith. Rokn Eddin had raised an army of 800,000 men, and was preparing to march against Georgia. Before setting out he sent an ambassador to the queen, asking her to renounce Christianity and become his wife, and concluding the letter with the threat that if she would not submit, he would come and make her his mistress. The ambassador who proposed such insolent terms would have been killed by Tamara's courtiers if she had not protected him. She wrote back calmly, expressing her trust in God, and declaring her determination to destroy Rokn Eddin and his infidel hosts. She finishes with a truly womanly touch: "Knowing how careless your men are, I do not return this by your messenger, but send one of my own servants with it."

Not contented with driving the Mahometans out of her own land, she sent ambassadors to the Christian communities in Alexandria, Libya, Mount Sinai, Jerusalem, Cyprus, Greece, and Rumania, to offer them help if they needed it; and in order to secure orthodoxy in the theology of her people, she commanded that a great disputation should be held between the doctors of the Georgian and Armenian Churches.

Her private life was not free from trouble. Three years after her accession she was prevailed upon to marry a Russian prince, Bogoliubovskoi, who had been driven out of his dominions in Muscovy. This individual conducted himself towards his consort in a shameful manner, and, after enduring his indignities for a long time, she complained to the ecclesiastical authorities, who granted her a divorce. She had no children by her first husband, so the nobles of the kingdom pressed her to marry again, in order that she might have an heir. Her beauty and her fame brought her suitors from the most distant lands. Mahometans renounced their religion for her, and there were many that died for love of her. She chose Prince David Soslan, an Osset, who, by his bravery and devotion, proved himself worthy to possess such a pearl among women, and she bore him a son, called Giorgi Lasha, in 1194, and a daughter, Rusudan, in 1195. Bogoliubovskoi, although he had been treated far beyond his deserts, twice invaded Georgia, but without success.

In 1212, wearied by her continual campaigns, and sorrow-stricken at the death of her husband and her greatest general, Tamara died, and left the throne to her son, *Giorgi Lasha*, at that time eighteen years of age. The young king was no sooner crowned than Ganja revolted, and this was soon followed by a still greater calamity, the invasion of Genghis Khan. Giorgi led 90,000 troops against the Mongols, but was defeated. In the meantime the Shah of Persia had asked for the hand of the beautiful Rusudan, and the Shah of Shirvan made a like demand.

Giorgi promised his sister to the latter, but he died in 1223.

Rusudan now became queen, and rejected both suitors in favour of Mogit Eddin, Lord of Erzerum. The Sultan of Khorassan thereupon desolated Georgia and took Tiflis, and the Persians and Mongols together made terrible havoc for a time. Rusudan at last submitted to the Mongols, and sent her son to the great Khan as a hostage. Georgia had now sunk very low indeed, and in 1243, on the death of Rusudan, her son, David IV., and her nephew, David V., divided the kingdom between them. Henceforth Kartli and Imereti were independent.

For the next 200 years we read of nothing but battles, sieges, raids, and in 1445 King Alexander completely destroyed the unity of the kingdom by dividing it among his three sons. He gave Kartli to Vakhtang, Imereti to Dimitri, Kakheti to Giorgi. In course of time Mingreli, Guri, Apkhazi, Svaneti, all revolted, and the land became the prey of Turks and Persians alternately, although even in its distracted condition, its people never lost their bravery, and were always respected by their enemies. Now and then the Mahometans succeeded in conquering one or other of the provinces, but it was never long before they were driven out again, and fire and sword carried into their own land.

Towards the end of the sixteenth century we find the country divided between the two great Mahometan powers, who had long made it their battle-field. Mingreli, Guri, Saatabago, and Imereti were held by the Turks; Kartli, Kakheti, Somkheti, and Kartuban voluntarily submitted to Persia, and were, in consequence, repeatedly devastated by the Tatar allies of the Ottoman Empire. In 1586 King Alexander II. of Kakheti sent ambassadors to the Tsar Feodor Ivanovich, asking for help, and a treaty was signed, according to which the Russian monarch agreed to protect Kakheti against the Turks, and to send troops to the Caucasus for this purpose. Shah Abbas the Great made no objection to this treaty, for he himself was anxious to gain the alliance of the Muscovites against Turkey.

Early in the seventeenth century King Giorgi of Kartli also sought Russian protection, and it is probable that Russia and Georgia would have been brought into very intimate connection by royal marriages, &c., if the death of Tsar Boris Godunov, and that of King Giorgi, who was poisoned by order of Shah Abbas, had not broken off the negotiations. The Persian Shah, suspecting King Alexander of Kakheti of a treasonable correspondence with the Turks, sent against him his (Alexander's) own son, Konstantin, who had been brought up at the Persian Court, and had embraced Islam. This apostate mercilessly killed his father and brother; but the nobles rose against him, and almost annihilated his army, whereupon he fled to the Lesghians, and offered to allow them to plunder Tiflis for three days if they would help him. They agreed. The nobles were defeated, and the land was again given up to the devastating infidels.

King Teimuraz of Kakheti, grandson of Alexander, in 1619, from a hiding-place in the mountains, sent an embassy to the Tsar Mikhail Feodorovich, beseeching him to have pity on his Georgian fellow-Christians. The Tsar requested Shah Abbas to cease from persecuting the Georgians, and his wish was granted in the most friendly way possible. Not only was Teimuraz allowed to return to Kakheti, but Kartli also was given to him, and remained a part of his kingdom until 1634, when it was taken from him and given to Rostom, a Mahometan. In 1653 Rostom took Kakheti also, and Teimuraz was obliged to seek refuge at the Court of Imereti, whence he proceeded to Moscow to ask for help;

but in consequence of the war then being waged against Poland, the Tsar could not spare any troops. Teimuraz returned to Georgia, and was taken prisoner by the Shah.

Imereti was at this time governed by King Bagrat, who came to the throne at the age of fifteen, his stepmother, Daredjan, being appointed regent. Daredjan endeavoured to gain the love of the young king, who was already married to her niece, and on his refusal to listen to her incestuous proposals, she had his eyes put out, and married Vakhtang Dshudshuna, whom she proclaimed king. Assisted by the Pasha of Akhaltsikhe, the loyal Imeretians replaced Bagrat the Blind on the throne, and then the eyes of Vakhtang were put out, and he and Daredjan were imprisoned.

On the death of Rostom, in 1658, Vakhtang IV., of the Mukhran family, became King of Kartli and Kakheti, and reigned till 1676. When he died his son Giorgi usurped the throne of Kartli, leaving only Kakheti to his elder brother Archil, who journeyed to Moscow, but did not get the desired aid from Russia. He then returned to the Caucasus, five times succeeded in obtaining the crown of Imereti, and five times was deposed. He died in Russia in 1713.

In 1703 Vakhtang V. came to the throne of Kartli. The first seven years of his reign were spent as a prisoner in Ispahan. In 1723 there was a fresh invasion of Turks, and, thinking his kingdom irrevocably lost, he fled to Russia, where he died.

Shah Nadir usurped the crown of Persia in 1736, and freed Kartli and Kakheti from the Turkish yoke. A little before his accession, in 1732, Russia had renounced in favour of Persia all right to the land between the Terek and the Kura. Nadir ingratiated himself with the Georgian nobility, and always gave them the post of honour in the victorious campaigns for which his reign is famous. Almost all the great warriors of the land accompanied him on his Indian march of conquest, and his especial favourite was *Irakli*, the son of Teimuraz, King of Kartli and Kakheti. An interesting story is told concerning the young warrior, in connection with this expedition. Kandahar having been taken in 1737, Nadir was marching towards Scinde, when he arrived at a certain column bearing an inscription which foretold death to those who went beyond it. Irakli, at that time only nineteen years of age, solved the difficulty by ordering the stone to be placed on the back of an elephant, which was led before the army. Scinde was conquered, and Irakli was richly rewarded. The Shah endeavoured to persuade the young prince to renounce the Christian religion, but neither threats nor caresses prevailed. India having been conquered, Nadir dismissed Irakli in 1739, and then invaded Central Asia, taking Balkh, Bokhara, Samarkand, whence he returned to the Caucasus and made war on the Lesghians. Irakli continued to distinguish himself by great bravery. On the Aragva he defeated 2000 Turks and Lesghians, was the first to cross the swollen river under a heavy musketry fire, and killed the leader of the enemy with his own hand. For this service Nadir bestowed upon him the kingdom of Kakheti in 1744.

In 1747 Shah Nadir was assassinated, and a period of anarchy began in Persia. Aga Mahmad Khan, the chief eunuch, usurped the dignity of Shah. Teimuraz and Irakli saved Erivan from the Persians in 1748, and this city paid tribute to Georgia until 1800, when the people, not wishing to fall into the hands of Russia, invited Persia to take the place. In 1749 Irakli, with 3000 men, signally defeated 18,000 Persians at Karaboulakh and again saved Erivan; then Ganja was taken, the Lesghians were dispersed, and an alliance was made with the Cherkesses. Teimuraz went to Russia in 1760; Tsaritsa Elizabeth received him with great honour, and promised to send troops to Georgia, but she died in 1761, and Teimuraz only survived her about a fortnight.

Irakli now succeeded to the throne of Kartli, and thus reunited this kingdom to Kakheti. The Catholicos Antoni, the most learned Georgian of his time, was recalled from exile in Russia and made patriarch; he founded at Tiflis and Telav schools where the " new philosophy " of Bacmeister was taught, translated many educational works into his native tongue, reformed the Church and encouraged literature.

A plot was formed against the king's life in 1765, under the following circumstances : Elizabeth, Irakli's sister, had been married for three years to a certain Giorgi, son of Dimitri Amilakhorishvili, who, for physical reasons, had been unable to consummate the marriage. Elizabeth applied for and obtained a divorce. Dimitri thought himself insulted in the person of his son, and he and his friends began to conspire with Paata, a natural son of Vakhtang V., who had been educated in Russia and England, and had just arrived in Georgia from the Persian court. Paata was to kill Irakli and proclaim himself king.

IRAKLI II

Page 124.

The conspiracy was discovered in time, and all those who had taken part in it were punished with death or mutilation.

Solomon, king of Imereti, had, in the meantime, been driven from his throne by the treachery of some of his nobles, who delivered Kutais, Shorapan and other fortresses to the Turks. He appealed to Catherine of Russia for help. Count Todleben arrived in the Caucasus with 5000 men in 1769, and Kutais was taken back, and Imereti freed from the oppression of the Turks. In the following year a great plague devastated the whole of Transcaucasia, 5000 died in Tiflis alone. The Holy Spear from the Armenian Convent at Edchmiadzin was brought out, and the plague ceased; whereupon the Lesghians demanded that the precious relic should be sent to them also; a spear was made exactly like the holy one, and it produced the same beneficent effect. Todleben was succeeded by Sukhotin, and in 1772, peace having been restored, the Russians returned homeward. But no sooner were they gone than the Turks again invaded Imereti; King Solomon, however, defeated them with great slaughter, killing many with his own hand.

Irakli's kingdom enjoyed comparative peace and prosperity for a time, and advantage was taken of this to disband the regular army and organize a militia, for the defence of the country against the raids of the irrepressible Lesghians. The king and his sons set an example to the people by subjecting themselves to the same discipline as private individuals, and those who did not present themselves for service were sought out and beaten with sticks. In 1779 the Khan of Erivan refused to pay tribute, and strongly fortified the city; the Georgians took the place and carried off several Armenians, who were removed to Tiflis, Gori, and Signakh, where they now constitute the trading and money-lending community.

In 1795 happened the terrible catastrophe which was to bring about the ruin of Georgia—the destruction of Tiflis by the Shah Aga Mahmad. The Persians marched through Armenia in great force, and reached the banks of the Kura without meeting with any serious opposition. Their advanced guard was attacked by the Georgians just outside the city, and was defeated on the 10th of September. Speaking of this battle, the Shah himself said, "I never saw so valorous a foe." On the following day the main body arrived, and Tiflis was taken by storm. King Irakli was so overcome with grief that he must have fallen into the hands of the enemy had not a few faithful nobles forcibly removed him from the captured city and conveyed him to Mtiuleti on the Aragva. Almost all the Georgian artillery, thirty-five guns, was taken, and the city and its environs were burnt to the ground.

For six days the work of destruction went on; women and young children were barbarously murdered, and the stench of rotting corpses made the place uninhabitable. A Persian historian says, "The brave Persian army showed the unbelieving Georgians what is in store for them at the day of judgment." All this havoc might have been prevented if Russia had sent the troops which she had solemnly promised by her treaties with Irakli, for the Shah had been making preparations for the invasion four months before it took place, and both Russia and Georgia were well aware of this.

Prince Giorgi, unworthy son of such a father, had been repeatedly ordered to bring his army to Tiflis, but he refused. No sooner did he hear of the fall of the capital than he prepared to flee from Signakh, although the place was strongly fortified, and there were many armed men there; but the inhabitants refused to let him go, and it was only by bribing his guards that he succeeded in escaping to Telav. Not one of Irakli's sons served him in the hour of his need.

Mtzkhet was captured and burnt, but the famous cathedral was spared, at the entreaty of the Khan of Nakhitshevan, who remonstrated against the desecration of the tomb of so many of Georgia's brave kings.

From Mtiuleti, Irakli proceeded to Ananur. The Shah sent after him 8000 men, guided by one of the king's own courtiers, but they were defeated. Aga Mahmad then offered to give up all the prisoners as well as the citadel of Tiflis if Irakli would renounce his treaty with Russia, and become tributary to Persia; but Irakli would not hear of any terms, however favourable, which would force him to be false to his alliance with Russia, although she, on her part, had forsaken him. He quickly assembled an army and marched to the southward, met the Persians between Kodjori and Krtsani and defeated them, re-taking Tiflis on the 6th of October.

A large Russian force now arrived and took Derbent, Shemakha, Baku, and several other fortresses in Daghestan, but the death of the Empress Catherine in 1796 put an end to the campaign, for Tsar Paul recalled all the troops from Transcaucasia. In 1797 Aga Mahmad Khan was again marching against Georgia, when he was fortunately assassinated, like his predecessor Nadir.

Plague and famine came to slay those who had escaped the sword of the Persians, and, worst of all, the great Irakli died in January, 1798, at the age of eighty, after a career almost unparalleled in history. Frederick of Prussia might well say, "Moi en Europe, et en Asie l'invincible Hercule, roi de Géorgie."

Giorgi now succeeded to the throne, and entered into negotiations with Persia, but Tsar Paul heard of the proposed alliance and outbid the Shah. A treaty was signed, confirming the throne to the Bagratid dynasty for ever, and promising military aid whenever it might be necessary. Alexander, the king's brother, now raised a revolt, which was put down with the help of the Russians; after all he had a grievance, for Irakli's will declared that he was to succeed Giorgi, while the Russians had persuaded the king to appoint as his heir his son David, a major-general in the Russian army. Alexander now appealed to Persia for aid, which he obtained, and in a three hours' battle at Kakabeti, on the Iora, he and Omar Khan, with an army of 12,000 men, were defeated. Giorgi died in 1800, and Georgia was then formally incorporated in the Russian empire.

General Knorring, the first governor, proceeded to the country with 10,000 men, and in the following year, under Tsar Alexander I., the annexation was confirmed. In 1803 Prince Tsitsishvili, a Georgian, succeeded Knorring. By his advice all the royal family were summoned to Russia, "in order to prevent civil dissensions," and this removal was accompanied by a very unfortunate incident. Queen Maria, widow of Giorgi, refused to go; General Lazarev proceeded early one morning to the queen's sleeping apartments with some soldiers and attempted to force her to accompany him; she killed him with a dagger which she had concealed under her dress, and her young son and daughter stabbed some of the soldiers. They were, of course, overpowered and carried off; at Dariel, in the narrowest part of the pass, a few Tagaur Ossets made a vain attempt at a rescue. Queen Maria was kept imprisoned in a convent at Voronezh for seven years, and never saw her native land again.

Tsitsishvili set himself to improve the condition of the country as much as possible. He began the military road over the Caucasus in 1804. He succeeded in persuading King Solomon of Imereti to acknowledge the Tsar as his suzerain, but Solomon soon began to intrigue with the Turks again. After taking Gandja by storm, and subduing a rising of the mountaineers under Pharnavaz and Iulon, sons of Irakli, Tsitsishvili marched against Baku, where he was treacherously murdered by the Khan of that city in 1806.

Count Gudovich was now appointed commander-in-chief, and his courtesy won for him the friendship of the Georgian people. Kakheti voluntarily submitted to his rule. He defeated the Turks in several battles, but was unsuccessful in his attack on Erivan, where he lost 2000 men. He was then recalled and made governor-general of Moscow. General Tormasov was the next ruler of Georgia, and he continued the war against the Turks, who were aided by King Solomon of Imereti. Poti was taken in 1810, and Princess Nina of Mingreli, who was allied to the Russians, herself led her troops to the assault. Sukhum was also taken. King Solomon was persuaded to go to a certain village in Kartli to sign a treaty of peace with Russia. The Russians treacherously seized him by night, and carried him off to prison in Tiflis, but he escaped in disguise, and fled to Akhaltsikhe, where he was received by the Turks with great honour. He returned to Imereti, and the whole country rose in his favour. There were revolts in Kakheti, and even among the Ossets, but they were soon crushed by force of numbers. Then came a plague which carried off vast numbers of victims in Imereti.

Tormasov was replaced by Paulucci, who, after a few months, was, in his turn, superseded by Rtishtshef. In 1813 took place the famous storming of Lenkoran, on the Caspian, by General Kotliarevski, followed by the Gulistan Treaty of Peace, which was signed on behalf of Persia by Sir Gore Ouseley, British ambassador at Teheran.

King Solomon died at Trebizond in 1815, and with him ended the troublous existence of Imereti as an independent kingdom. In about three and a half centuries thirty kings had sat on the Imeretian throne, twenty-two of them were dethroned (one of them, Bagrat the Blind, eight times), seven died a violent death, three were blinded.

Yermolov became governor-general in 1816, and soon afterwards the Chechens and Daghestanians began to give the Russians serious trouble. Then the clergy raised a national movement in Imereti, in which Guri and Apkhazi joined, and in Mingreli, hitherto faithful, the Dadian's brother revolted. All these efforts to shake off the Russian yoke were, of course, fruitless, and they ended in 1822 with the capture of

Zakatali from the Lesghians. Then the Cherkesses (Circassians) broke into rebellion, and in 1826 Persia again declared war against Russia and marched 60,000 men into Georgia. Aided by the Lesghians and the Kakhetians, under Alexander, son of Irakli, they were at first successful, but the tide turned, and Erivan, Tavriz, and other places saw Russia victorious.

Paskevich succeeded Yermolov in 1827, and the peace of Turkmenchai having been concluded with Persia, war was declared against Turkey. The Russians took Kars, Poti, Akhalkalaki, Akhaltsikhe, Bayazid from the Turks, and in 1829 the belligerents signed the treaty of Adrianople.

In 1830 Kasi-mullah began his revolt, and brought about a general rising among the Mahometan peoples of the Caucasus. Baron Rosen, who took the command of the army in 1831, captured Gimri, and Kasi-mullah was killed. Golovin (1837), Neidhart (1842), and Prince Vorontsov (1844—1854) enjoyed comparative peace, and were able to turn their attention to the internal condition of the country. Prince Vorontsov especially deserves credit for his honest and painstaking efforts to ameliorate the economic situation of Georgia, and it flatters our national pride to remember that that statesman was English by birth and education, if not by blood.

The pacification of Daghestan did not, as was expected, follow the death of Kasi-mullah. A greater prophet and warrior arose to take the place of the vanquished hero of Gimri. Shamil, after carrying on a guerilla warfare for about ten years, raised the whole of the Eastern Caucasus in 1843, and continued to inflict a series of crushing defeats on the Russian generals who were sent to oppose him. The declaration of war with Turkey in 1853 raised the hopes of the Lesghians, but the utter incapacity of the Turkish leaders in Armenia prevented the realization of those hopes. Everybody is familiar with the incidents of Shamil's career down to the capture at Gunib in 1859; but it seems to me that too little attention has been devoted to the remarkable religious system which inspired the Murids to their marvellous deeds of valour. It is surely a noteworthy fact that the mysticism of the Sufis should have been found to be compatible with a purely militant faith like Islam.

During the last thirty years little of interest has happened in Georgia. The appointment of the Grand Duke Mikhail Nikolaevich to the lieutenancy of the Caucasus in 1862, the gradual freeing of the serfs, the construction of railway and telegraph lines of communication, the founding of one or two banks, schools, and other establishments of public utility, are the chief events which the annalist has to chronicle. "Free" Svaneti was conquered a few years ago, and, for the present, Russia's supremacy is undisputed as far as the frontiers of Turkev and Persia. Even the last war between Russia and Turkey was not accompanied by any visible commotion among the peoples of the Caucasus.

There is as yet no *history* of Georgia in the sense in which we now understand the word. Those works which are dignified with the name are merely more or less trustworthy collections of materials, which in their present form produce only a feeling of bewilderment in the reader. We trust that a man worthy of the task will seriously take the annals of his nation in hand, and present them to the world in an intelligible form; and we also cherish the hope that he will not finish his task without being able to chronicle the new birth of a strong, independent state worthy to maintain the fame of Irakli and Tamara.

THE LANGUAGE AND LITERATURE OF GEORGIA.

The origin of the Kartlian or Kartvelian language is still involved in some doubt, but the general opinion of philologists seems to be that it does not belong to the Indo-European family, although it has been powerfully influenced by Zend, Sanskrit, Persian, and Armenian. The ancient speech of the country is preserved to us in the ecclesiastical rituals and books of devotion, which are written in characters differing very considerably from the civil alphabet, the "war hand," the invention of the latter being ascribed to King Pharnavaz I., a contemporary of Alexander the Great. The *Khutsuri*, or ecclesiastical character, bears a striking resemblance to Armenian; an excellent specimen of it may be seen in the British Museum Library, in the famous Moscow Bible of 1743, recently purchased. The number of letters is the same in both alphabets, viz. thirty-eight, and the modern alphabet is as follows :—

THE LANGUAGE AND LITERATURE OF GEORGIA.

ა	a	ს	
ბ	b	ტ	
გ	g	უ	u (oo)
დ	d	ვ	vi (vee)
ე	e	ფ	ph (p followed by sound of h)
ვ		ქ	k
ზ	z	ღ	gh (guttural)
ც	é (short)	ყ	(something like a guttural k)
თ	th (not English *th* but t followed by sound of h)	შ	sh
ი	i (English *ee*)	ჩ	ch
კ	c; k	ც	tz
		ძ	dz
		წ	ts
მ	m	ჭ	dch
ნ	n	ხ	kh
ჲ	i (short)	ჴ	khh
ო		ჯ	j
პ	p	ჰ	h
ჟ	zh		ho
რ			

The orthography is purely phonetic. There is very little difference between the language of the sacred books and that of to-day, not nearly so much as between Anglo-Saxon and English; but many foreign words have been introduced in modern times.

The earliest specimens of Georgian literature which have come down to us are translations of the Scriptures, and theological works written under the influence of the Greek clergy, who, until the eleventh century, occupied almost all the high ecclesiastical offices in the land.

In the eleventh and twelfth centuries of our era the relations between Georgia and Greece were of the most intimate character. The young nobles of the court of King David the Renewer and his immediate successors frequented the schools of Athens, and brought back with them Platonic and Aristotelian teachings which exerted a very powerful influence on the intellectual and social life of that period, and prepared the way for the golden age of Georgian literature, which dawned on the accession of Queen Tamara. Sulkhan Orbeliani, in the preface to his dictionary, compiled early in the eighteenth century, says that he consulted translations of Proklus, Platonicus, Nemesis, Aristotle, Damascenus Plato, Porphyry, and many other Greek writers. If these MSS. were still extant, they might prove valuable to classical scholars.

UNIV. OF
CALIFORNIA

RUSTAVELI

Page 139

During the stormy times that soon followed, the countless lyrical pieces which were produced were nearly all lost, but the epic which is now looked upon as the greatest masterpiece in the language has escaped with but a few mutilations. This is "The Man in the Panther's Skin" (Vepkhvis Tkaosani) by *Shota Rustaveli*.

History tells us very little about Shota Rustaveli. We only know that he was born in the village of Rustavi, near Akhaltsikhe, that he received his education in Athens, returned to his native land, where he wrote his great work, was secretary to Queen Tamara, then became a monk, and died in the monastery of the Holy Cross, near Jerusalem, where his portrait may still be seen. Tradition says that the poet was passionately enamoured of his royal mistress, and this assertion seems to be borne out by many passages in the poem.

During nearly seven centuries of ceaseless struggles for freedom, the Georgians have kept this great work fresh in their minds. It has inspired them with hope and courage in the darkest hours, and at the present day it is as great a favourite as it ever was. Not only are many of its verses household words in cottage and hall, but there are not a few Georgians, especially among the women, who know every word of it by heart; indeed, there was a time when no woman was allowed to marry unless she could repeat the whole poem. The reason for this extraordinary popularity is to be found in the fact that the poem is a thoroughly national one in its smallest details. Although the heroes and heroines are described as Arabians, Indians, Chinese, they are all Georgians to the very finger tips.

The plot is of the simplest description possible. Rostevan, a patriarchal Eastern king, who has renounced the throne of Arabia in favour of his daughter Tinatina, is out hunting one day with Avtandil, one of his generals, when he sees a weeping youth of wondrous beauty, dressed in a panther's skin. The king orders his guards to seize the stranger, but the latter kills several of them and mysteriously escapes, whereupon the old king falls into a fit of sadness so deep that Tinatina at length promises her hand to the knight who will satisfy her father's curiosity. Avtandil sets out to seek the man in the panther's skin, wanders about for three years, meeting with wondrous adventures, before he finds the object of his search, who turns out to be Tariel, a young knight enamoured of Nestan Daredjan, daughter of the king of

India, and then returns to claim the hand of his queen.

In Avtandil we have a Christian chevalier of the East who is worthy of comparison with our Rolands and Red Cross Knights, while Tariel is a wild Mussulman, whose passion drives him to excesses worthy of Amadis of Gaul.

The interest is powerfully sustained all through the poem, and its dramatic unity is never lost sight of; yet, however interesting the narrative may be, it is chiefly as a picture of life in Georgia in the days of Tamara that "The Man in the Panther's Skin" is valuable.

Tinatina, who is none other than Tamara herself, is described as follows:—

> "One daughter only had the aged king,
> And she was fair as is the Eastern sun.
> He upon whom her gaze but once did rest
> Was ravish'd of his heart and soul and thought."

Tinatina is a beautiful type of womanhood, such as we might expect to find in the literature of Western Europe, but hardly in a little country standing alone amid the wild hordes of Asia. Her wisdom, her strength of character, the purity and loyalty of her love, have made her the model of many a generation of Rustaveli's countrywomen, who have ever behaved nobly alike in joy and sorrow.

Avtandil is thus portrayed:—

> "A prince's son was Avtandil, the very first
> 'Mong all the bravest warriors of the aged king
> His form was slender as the cypress-tree,
> And clear and beauteous was his piercing glance.
> Though young, his soul was true and strong
> As adamant is hard.
> The fire from Tinatina's eyes had long
> Set his young heart aflame with strong desire,
> And stricken him with wounds that never heal'd.
> Many a day he hid his burning love,
> And sunder'd from his mistress, all the red
> Fled from his roselike, tender cheeks;
> But soon as fate did bring him near to her again,
> The wildly beating heart crimson'd his face,
> And all his aching wounds did gape afresh.
> Thus hidden love doth torture youthful breasts."

From "The Man in the Panther's Skin" we learn that the ideal hero of Rustaveli's times was distinguished for bravery, truthfulness, loyalty to promises, self-sacrifice, munificence, and burning love.

> "Falsehood's the root of all the thousand ills
> That curse our race. Lying and faithlessness twin sisters are.
> Why should I try to cheat my fellow-man?
> Is this the use to which my learning should be put?
> Ah, no! far other aims our hearts inspire,
> We learn, that we may near the angelic choir."

The most famous line in the whole poem is, perhaps, the one which says :—

"A glorious death is better than a life of shame."

And many a warrior has sought death, in the hour of defeat, with these words on his lips.

Another verse which has become proverbial is ·—

"That which thou dost on other's wants bestow, is thine,
While that thou hoardest is all lost to thee."

The ideas of love expressed by Rustaveli are partly of the Ovidian type, without any of the indelicacy of the Latin poet. But he had not studied Plato for nought, and we see in his work traces of those metaphysical theories which S. Bonaventura, Dante, and many of their contemporaries and successors found in Christianity

In the last strophe we have a prophecy, conscious or unconscious, of the evil days that were about to dawn.

"Their deeds are ended, like a dream at night.
With them their golden age has ended too.
Far other days have dawn'd.
Such is that old deceiver Time ; he makes
That which at first did everlasting seem
As short as is the twinkling of an eye."

As far as style is concerned, we find that Rustaveli strikingly resembles the European writers of his own time, to wit the troubadours, and we can easily imagine that his career was not unlike that of some of those sweet singers who enjoyed the favour of the noble ladies of France and Italy. Among the great poets of Europe, Ariosto and Tasso are, perhaps, the ones who are most akin to Rustaveli. The Platonism of the latter furnishes another ground of resemblance, in addition to the similarity of theme.

The poem in its present form consists of about 1600 quatrains. There are sixteen syllables in each line, and the four lines end with the same rhyme. The rhythm is due to the accents, as in English verse, and may be called hexametric, i.e. there are in each line six feet, divided into two sets of three by means of the cæsura; the fourth line invariably begins with the particle *i*, which does not count as a syllable.

As far as I know, the poem has not been translated into any European language; although fragments and abstracts of it have been published in Russian and Polish magazines, and I have seen the name of "Rostavvelo" quoted in one of Gioberti's works. By the publication of a carefully collated text, about a year ago, Georgian critics have prepared the way for those who may wish to make the national epic known to European readers.

Among the contemporaries of Rustaveli may be mentioned the following:—

Chakhrukhadze, the author of the " Tamariani," a long poem in honour of Queen Tamara; it is composed entirely of epithets, thus —

> "Tamartsknari, shesatsknari, khmanarnari, pirmtsinari,
> Mse mtsinari, sachinari, tskalimknari, momdinari,"

i.e.

> "Tamara, the mild, the pleasing, the sweetly speaking, the kindly smiling,
> The sunlike shining one, the majestic, the gently moving, like a full river."

Shavteli was even more highly prized than Rustaveli, but his greatest work is lost. *Khoneli* and *Tmokveli*, the former in "Daredjaniani," the latter in "Visramiani" and "Dilariani," have left us romances of chivalry and adventure which are still much admired, and are well worthy of comparison with the best European literature of the same class. About the same time the national chronicle, called "Kartlis tzkhovreba," i.e. Georgia's Life, was written.

This period of literary activity was brought to an abrupt close by the terrible invasion of Genghis Khan, and for about four centuries the incessant wars in which the country was engaged gave plenty of opportunity for acting romances, but little time for writing them.

Towards the end of the seventeenth century *Prince Sulkhan Orbeliani* described his "Journey through Europe," and wrote a collection of fables and folk-tales, lately published in Russian. Orbeliani had lived at the court of Louis XIV., and was very friendly with La Fontaine, who is indebted to the Georgian prince for some of his fables. His greatest service to his country was, however, the compilation of a dictionary, containing 25,000 words, which has formed the basis for all later lexicographical works.

In 1712 King Vakhtang VI. opened a printing office in Tiflis, and issued the chief poems and romances of the Tamarian period at such a price as to make them attainable by all his subjects. Irakli II., of glorious memory, continued to act as the Augustus of Georgian literature, and in the Catholicos Antoni it found a Mæcenas or Pollio. The chief writers of the eighteenth century were *Prince Vakhusht*, son of Vakhtang VI., who compiled a "History of Georgia" and a "Geography of Georgia," and the *Catholicos Antoni*, who published many educational and religious works. *Guramoshvili* and *Savatnava* sang the triumphs of

Irakli in powerful lyrics which are still familiar to every peasant.

The following serenade belongs to this period; it was copied down by Pushkin in 1829, and he says of it, " There is in it a certain Oriental inconsequence which is not altogether devoid of poetical worth."

> " Soul newly born in Paradise!
> Soul made for my delight!
> From thee, thou deathless one,
>   I wait for life.
> From thee, thou flowery springtide, moon but two weeks old,
> From thee, my guardian angel,
>   I wait for life.
> With joyous smiles thy face doth shine.
> I would not change thy glance against the throne of all the world.
>   From thee I wait for life.
> Rose of the mountain, wet with the dew of dawn!
> Nature's chief favourite! Hidden treasure house!
>   From thee I wait for life."

It was not, however, until the present century was well begun, that Georgian poetry abandoned the " Oriental inconsequence " to which I have just referred; the literary awakening which began about sixty or seventy years ago was largely due to the work of Western poets, such as Byron, with whom the Georgians became familiar chiefly through Pushkin and Lermontov. *Prince Alexander Chavchavadze* (1786—1846), a general in the Russian service, was the founder of the modern school; his song is all of love and wine. The influence of Western romanticism is still more clearly visible in the earlier productions of *Baratashvili* (1816—1846), but he succeeded in throwing off the gloomy misanthropy of his youth, and had the courage to acknowledge that he had been deluded by that " evil spirit " of Byronism.

To *Prince Giorgi Eristavi* fell the task of familiarizing his countrymen with the poetical literature of Europe. He was exiled to Poland for his share in a plot against the Russian government, and spent his leisure in studying Mickiewicz, Schiller, Petrarch, and Pushkin, selections from whose works he published in his native tongue. On his return to Tiflis he founded a National Theatre, for which he himself wrote many comedies. With Eristavi sentimentalism died, and the poets who succeeded him sought inspiration in patriotic ideals.

Prince Grigor Orbeliani (1801—1883), sang the past splendour of his fatherland, and bewailed the low estate to which it had fallen. In his " Ode to Tamara's portrait " he beseeches the great queen to look down with pity on Georgia, and bless her sons with strength and wisdom; he despairingly asks:—

> "Shall that which once was wither'd, ne'er again
> Enjoy the fragrance of its former bloom?
> Shall that which fell, for ever fallen remain,
> O'erwhelm'd in an unchanging, cruel doom?"

His lines on the death of Irakli II. breathe the same spirit:—

> "Ah! full of splendour were the fateful days
> That saw the quenching of thy quickening light,
> Thou sun of Georgia, yet thy dazzling rays
> Still lighten up the darkness of our night.
>
> "Thine all-o'erpowering sword, whose mighty blows
> Scatter'd like chaff the bravest of the brave,
> Shall never more affright thy country's foes
> Georgia's fame lies buried in thy grave."

Orbeliani had a warm heart for the poor and suffering, and his "Lopiana the Fisherman" and "Bokuladze the Musha" (a *musha* is a carrier of heavy burdens) are masterpieces in their way.

While Orbeliani's eyes are ever turned regretfully to the past, *Akaki Tsereteli* (born 1840) looks hopefully forward to the future:—

> "Ah no! our love is not yet dead,
> It only sleeps awhile . . . . . ."

In elegant yet forcible lyrics he invites his countrymen to manfully follow the path of progress. Tsereteli has written a great historical poem called "Torniki," and is, besides, an orator and publicist of the first rank.

Of the same school is *Prince Ilia Chavchavadze* (born 1837), who is in many respects the most remarkable man that Georgia possesses. All his poems, and indeed all his work, whether as a poet, a novelist, a journalist, an orator, or a financier, breathe a spirit of the loftiest patriotism. The return of spring and the awakening of bird and flower to fuller life are to him a reminder of the long-delayed awakening of his beloved land; his elegies on the Kura, the Aragva, the Alazana are all full of the same feeling. It is, however, in "Lines to the Georgian mother" that he most clearly expresses his ideas; after reminding the matrons of Georgia how they have served their country in times past, cheerfully sending their sons forth to the fight and sustaining their courage in the hour of misfortune, he says :—

". . . But why should we shed idle tears
For glory that will ne'er return?
The ever-flowing stream of years
Leaves us no time to idly mourn.

" 'Tis ours to tread an untried path,
'Tis ours the future to prepare.
If forward thou dost urge thy sons,
Then answer'd is my earnest prayer.

> "This is the task that waits for thee,
> Thou virtuous mother of our land,
> Strengthen thy sons, that they may be
> Their country's stay with heart and hand.
>
> "Inspire them with fraternal love,
> Freedom, equality and right,
> Teach them to struggle 'gainst all ill
> And give them courage for the fight."

Chavchavadze's tales and poems have done more than anything else to awaken the Georgian people to a sense of the duties they have to perform in the altered conditions under which they now live. His poem, "Memoirs of a Robber," which portrayed the lazy country squires who lived on the toil of their serfs, made a powerful impression on the class it was meant for; and the tale, "Is that a man?" which describes the life of a young noble who spends his whole time in eating, drinking, sleeping and folly, brought a blush to the faces of hundreds of his countrymen, and prompted them to seek a worthier mode of existence. At first, the more conservative part of the nobility were bitterly opposed to the radical ideas of Chavchavadze, but he has now succeeded in bringing round the majority of them to his way of thinking. He is editor of a daily paper, *Iveria*, which is read by all classes of society, and most of his time is spent between his journalistic duties and the management of the nobles' Land Bank, an institution founded for the relief of the farmers.

Besides those I have mentioned, Chavchavadze has written many other works; with the following extract from "The Phantom" I conclude this brief notice of him:—

"O Georgia, thou pearl and ornament of the world. What sorrow and misfortune hast thou not undergone for the Christian faith! Tell me, what other land has had so thorny a path to tread? Where is the land that has maintained such a fight twenty centuries long without disappearing from the earth? Thou alone, Georgia, couldst do it. No other people can compare with thee for endurance. How often have thy sons freely shed their blood for thee! Every foot of thy soil is made fruitful by it. And even when they bowed under oppression they always bravely rose again. Faith and freedom were their ideals."

The novel of social life is represented by *Prince Kazbek*, a young and energetic writer, many of whose productions have appeared as serials in the newspapers. The best writer of historical novels is *Rtsheuli*; his "Queen Tamara" is a great favourite with the people.

The National Theatre is kept well supplied with

PRINCE ILIA CHAVCHAVADZE.

PRINCE IVANÉ MACHABELI.
Page 152.

TO MY
CHILDREN

new and original comedies by *Tsagareli* and others, and *Prince Ivané Machabeli*, who, as far as I know, is the only Georgian who can read English literature in the original, has translated some of Shakspeare's plays; these always draw a full house, and are thoroughly appreciated. Leaving out of the question "King Lear," which has a special interest for the people, on account of its reminding them of Irakli II., this hearty admiration for Shakspeare is somewhat remarkable; in my opinion it is to be explained by the fact that the Georgian people are in almost the same state of intellectual and social development as were our forefathers in the days of Queen Elizabeth, and they can, therefore, the more fully enter into our great poet's way of thinking. Besides the essential part of his work, the effect of which on the minds of men will always be the same, there is an accessory part, a tone, an atmosphere, which more particularly belongs to the early part of a period of transition from feudalism to freedom, from faith to rationalism, from the activity of war to the activity of peace; ten or a dozen generations have lived in England since this stage in our history was reached; in Georgia there still live men who were born in the age of chivalry and adventure.

Prince Machabeli, in spite of the fact that he

is only about thirty years of age, is, perhaps, after Prince Ilia Chavchavadze, the man who enjoys the greatest influence among his fellow-countrymen. His studies at the University of Paris, and his intimate acquaintance with the intellectual and social life of Europe, have enabled him to bring the younger generation at least to a fuller appreciation of the superiority of the West over the East; everything which savours of Asia is now rigidly proscribed or ridiculed, and Romano-Germanic ideals prevail. As the editor of *Droeba* (Time), a capital daily paper, Macha beli had an opportunity of spreading his opinions throughout the country, but an imprudent article brought about the suppression of the journal by the Censure.

This notice would be incomplete without a brief reference to the venerable *Bishop Gabriel* of Kutais, whose homilies are at once elegant in style and simple in doctrine; they have had a very powerful influence on the Georgian people, and their author is sincerely loved by all his countrymen. An English translation of his earlier sermons has been published by the Rev. S. C. Malan.

The popular literature of Georgia is rich in folk-tales, fables, ballads, riddles, &c., and would well repay an attentive study (v. Bibliography).

BISHOP GABRIEL OF KUTAIS.   Page 154.

THE POLITICAL CONDITION OF THE KINGDOM OF GEORGIA.

It is well known that there are within the Russian frontiers peoples not inferior in historical importance or intellectual development to the regnant race, and we might reasonably suppose that Russophobes would give us some information about those nations which would probably be their allies in the struggle which they profess to consider inevitable Yet the course of action likely to be adopted by Poland, Finland, or Georgia, in case of an Anglo-Russian war, is hardly ever discussed, and when a passing reference is made to the matter, the most erroneous ideas are expressed.

As far as I know, the only living English statesman who knows anything at all about the condition of the Caucasus, is Professor James Bryce, who, in a work published in 1877, records the impressions received during a short visit made in the previous year. His remarks are interesting in the highest degree, and exhibit a rare keenness of insight; yet that part of them which refers more particularly to Georgia is open to three very serious objections.

1. The shortness of the author's stay forced him to come to conclusions which a longer experience would have modified very considerably. He himself frankly acknowledged this in many places.

2. Mr. Bryce did not come into contact with any prominent Georgians; he was, therefore, obliged to depend upon foreigners for information about the political condition of the country and the aspirations of the native population. This is why he said so little about Georgia in the last chapter of his book. In that chapter the place of honour is reserved for the Armenians, whose recognized champion our illustrious fellow-countryman has now become.

3. There has, of late, been a great change in the country. The Georgia of to-day is not the Georgia of 1876. Certain causes, which will be touched upon in the present article, have, in the meantime, brought about an awakening as sudden as it is complete.

There is one Englishman who could accurately describe the political condition of Transcaucasia, and it is a subject for congratulation that he is Her Majesty's Vice-Consul at Batum. When the British Government wakes up to a recognition of the fact that we have interests to protect in the region between the Black Sea and the Caspian, the consulate in Tiflis (abolished in 1881, " because the objects for which it was founded were not accomplished ") may, perhaps, be re-established, and in that case no more able and sympathetic consul could be chosen than Mr. D. R. Peacock, who for so many years has upheld the honour of our flag in the fever-stricken swamps of Poti and Batum.

The writer of the present article is well aware of his unfitness for the task he has set himself, yet he feels sure that the result of his unprejudiced observation cannot fail to be interesting; if he only succeeds in provoking adverse criticism he will be satisfied, for thereby attention will be drawn to a question the discussion of which must lead to a far better understanding of many points of vital importance.

At the very outset it is necessary to remove from the mind of the reader an opinion which is almost universally held in Europe, and which is, perhaps, the chief cause of that apathy with which politicians look upon the Caucasus. It is generally believed, even by some of those who have been in the country, that Transcaucasia is inhabited by a vast number of tribes, more or less wild, having nothing in common but the doubtful benefits of Russian rule. Nothing could be more misleading. Students of ethnography may amuse themselves by making elaborate investigations into the origin and characteristics of the Khevsur, the Svan, the Pshav, the Osset, it is sufficient for us to know that all these peoples are, politically at least, Georgians, and have fought under the Kartvelian kings since the days of William the Conqueror. Between the Caucasus, the Black Sea, the Caspian, and the frontiers of Turkey and Persia, there are only three native peoples who deserve our consideration, viz. :—

The various Lesghian tribes in the E., numbering about ... 1,500,000
The Armenians, in the S., numbering about 740,000
The Georgians, in the W., ,, over 1,000,000

The latter total is made up as follows :—

(*a*) Kartlians, Kakhetians, and Ingiloitsi 310,000
(*b*) Highlanders, i.e. Khevsurs, Pshavs, Tushes 20,000
(*c*) Imeretians and Gurians 380,000
(*d*) Adjartsi, Kobuletsi (in valleys near Artvin) 46,000
(*e*) Mingrelians 200,000

(*f*) Lazes (near Batum). The majority
are still in Turkey ...   2,000
(*g*) Svans   12,000

To these may be added :—

The Apkhazi (near Sukhum)   32,000

and

The Ossets (south of the Caucasus)   53,000

There are also many Georgians in Turkey, and a few in Persia. The numerous local appellations given above mean no more than Yorkshireman, Cornishman, or Aberdonian do to us. If I succeed in impressing upon my readers the fact that *there is a politically homogeneous region stretching from the steppe of Baku to the Black Sea,* my labour will not have been fruitless.

It is a significant fact that the pure Georgian language is now far more generally spoken than it has been for many centuries, and that the dialects are rapidly disappearing. This is due in a great measure to the growth of a taste for literature, which is fostered by the newspapers and other periodical publications. There are, besides, many schools where the language is taught, for the Georgians have hitherto escaped the fate of the Armenians, whose schools were closed after the recent insurrection, and a society exists in Tiflis for the dissemination of the national literature among the peasants. All this has helped to produce a national feeling, stronger than any that has existed since the fatal partition of the kingdom in the fifteenth century. The petty jealousies between Kartlian, Kakhetian and Imeretian have been forgiven and forgotten, and when Georgia's voice is again heard in Asia she will speak with that authority which belongs only to a united, patriotic people.

In order to understand the state of political feeling in Georgia during the present century, it is necessary to remember what her previous history has been. During a long period, stretching back to ages of which we have only fragmentary records, the country had ever been at war; often conquered, still more often conquering, never crushed, this brave little state maintained its existence for a thousand years, alone in the very midst of those fierce fanatics whose fame made all allied Europe quake. At length, rent by civil war and ravaged by the infidel, it wisely resolved to throw itself into the hands of a Christian power able and willing to protect and avenge. After availing themselves of Russia's help, it was but natural that the Georgians should seek the repose of which they were so much in need; and, though they were ever ready to fight against the common foe, yet, with a few praiseworthy exceptions, they busied themselves little with the internal administration of their land. Indeed, there was no call for such interference as long as they were under the mild and beneficent rule of that ideal Tsar, Alexander I., represented by such worthy lieutenants as Tsitsishvili and Yermolov. They continued to live thus contentedly and, it must be confessed, lazily for about two generations; only ten years ago it used to be said in Tiflis, "If you see a shopkeeper asleep, he is sure to be a Georgian." This sleepiness is now at an end. Opinions may differ as to the cause of the awakening; harsh measures on the part of Russia, whose policy in Transcaucasia has been becoming more and more irritating ever since the removal of Prince Vorontsov, in 1854, and culminating last year in the enforcement of military service, have undoubtedly had some effect of this kind, but unless there had been a simultaneous progress in the intellectual and social development of the nation, this overbearing legislation might have been sullenly submitted to without complaint.

There can be little doubt of the fact that the excessive precautions taken by the police, with a view to put down political agitation of any kind, have produced the very thing they are intended to prevent. A country squire in talking to me, one day, about a little market-town near his home, said, "They have posted a gendarme there. Until he came nobody ever bothered about politics. Now there is nothing else talked of." Some time ago the young Georgian nobles who were serving in the Russian army became infected with the doctrines of revolutionary socialism, and not a few suffered for their imprudence (e.g. the famous Tsitsianov, in 1877); at the present time the national feeling has become so strong as to leave no room for these ideas. Nevertheless, during my stay in Tiflis, last summer, a rumour was rife to the effect that a large number (a hundred or two) of young noblemen were about to be exiled, in view of the visit of the Tsar, who was expected to arrive at his new palace at Tsinondal, near Telav, in the autumn. The fact that this report was believed by the parties interested, is a powerful testimony to the arbitrary character of the proceedings of the Russian police.

In the rural districts the people only know Russia as a foreign power that sends them tax-collectors, justices of the peace, and other civil servants, who perform obnoxious functions in a manner not calculated to conciliate the ratepayers. It is notorious that the *chinovnik* has an unpleasant reputation, even among his fellow-countrymen, and those who consent to a temporary exile in Transcaucasia are not precisely the flower of the profession, although their behaviour to Europeans leaves little to be desired. The justices of the peace, as in Poland, are directly appointed by the Minister of Justice at Petersburg; all the evidence has to be translated into the official language, and this accentuates the natural feeling of the litigants that they are being tried by foreign laws arbitrarily imposed from without. The personal character of the judges is, in many cases, not such as to inspire respect for the law; the arrogant, bullying tone of these personages is intolerable at any time, but especially when aggravated by alcoholism. I shall never forget one scene in particular at which I was present; a fine, tall mountaineer came humbly to present a petition to a puny, besotted judge, who was a guest at the house where I was staying; the representative of law and order was drunk, hopelessly drunk, and treated the suppliant in such a manner that I blushed to be in his company; I feared that the petitioner would take summary revenge for the insult, but he restrained his wrath; as he turned away there was on his face a look of hellish hatred, and I do not think that he will trouble the court again as long as he has a sharp *kinjal* of his own wherewith to settle disputes.

Whatever may be the cause of the awakening, there cannot be any doubt of its reality. Nevertheless, it is hard to give any definite description of the channels into which the national activity is finding its way. In any case it may be safely said that the Georgian people are not likely to imitate the imprudent conduct of their neighbours the Armenians, who have, more than once, unseasonably provoked popular movements which they had not the power to bring to a happy issue. The character of the Georgians is too frank and open for the hatching of plots; however strong their feelings may be, they know how to wait until an opportunity arrives for the satisfaction of those feelings; the perfect unanimity in the aims of the people renders an elaborate organization unnecessary

It is interesting to notice that the political ideals of the country are borrowed from Western Europe. Excepting in Japan, perhaps, there is no such instance of a people passing directly from feudalism to liberalism. The grandsons of absolute monarchs, the men who little more than a quarter of a century ago were large slaveholders, are now ardent champions of the democratic idea, and loudly proclaim the freedom, the equality, the brotherhood, of prince and peasant, master and man. This is not the only case in which Georgia has turned her back on Asia and opened her arms to Europe—Parisian fashions, German rationalism, English sport and other products of our civilization are beginning to have an influence; however, it is a consolation to remember that the women, in every country the more Conservative and, at the same time, more patriotic half of the community, may be counted upon to restrain their husbands and sons from a too hasty advance in the slippery paths of modern progress.

It must not be supposed that the Georgian people are forgetful of what Russia has done for them in protecting them against Persia and Turkey; they have no hatred for their Slav fellow subjects, indeed, it is hard to imagine how any one could dislike such an amiable individual as the average Russian, not being an official; but on the other hand, it must be remembered that this military aid is the only benefit Georgia has ever received. It is true that roads have been made, but their construction was only undertaken in order to facilitate the movement of troops, and they are practically worthless for the purposes of trade. The industrial and commercial development of the country has been wholly neglected; and, at the instigation of the late editor of the *Moscow News*, the transit of foreign merchandise was prohibited. At the present time a few Russian capitalists are endeavouring to get a footing beyond the Caucasus, but they experience some difficulty in doing so, for the Georgians prefer to avail themselves of the services of European investors; among others, the Rothschilds have not been slow to see that Transcaucasian wines, ores and oils are worth attention.

Should Russia ever become involved in a great war, Georgia would undoubtedly declare her independence, and endeavour to seize the Dariel Road; the Armenians and Lesghians would also revolt, each in their own way. It is idle to speculate as to the result of such a movement, but it may interest the reader to know that it took an army of more than a quarter of a million men to conquer the Lesghians alone, in the time of Shamil. The Russians put so little confidence in the loyalty of their Caucasian army, that they took care to send a large part of it to Poland in January last, when there seemed to be a prospect of war with

Austria. This was a prudent measure; but, after all, it does not matter so very much whether Georgian soldiers mutiny in Georgia or Poland, Poles in Poland or Georgia, the essential point at which diplomats hostile to Russia would aim is, of course, to bring about perfectly simultaneous action on the part of all the enemies of that power, both at home and abroad. It is superfluous to add that the Georgian troops are the flower of the Russian army; every schoolboy can ride and shoot like a trained man; their officers are especially good, and there are at present many generals who are worthy successors of Andronikov, Bagration and Loris Melikov

The sympathy with which the Armenian national movement has been regarded in Western Europe encourages the Georgians to hope that a like feeling will be manifested towards them when the time is ripe for action. It is especially upon England that their hopes are fixed, for they are well aware of the fact that the existence of a strong, independent state between the Black Sea and the Caspian would be an enormous advantage to our country. The possibility of Armenians, Georgians and Lesghians consenting to combine into one homogeneous state is not to be thought of; but there is no reason why the descendants of the three sons of Targamos, great-great-grandson of Noah, should not, if they were free, form a defensive alliance for the protection of common interests; the Lesghians have, in past times, done good service against both Persians and Turks. In any case, Georgia has a frontier which she is quite able to defend, and she could always count upon the assistance of the mountaineers on the northern side of the Caucasus. The Cherkesses (Circassians), whose hatred of Russia is well known, have almost all migrated to Asia Minor.

It is sincerely to be hoped that the present good feeling between the Georgian and Russian peoples may continue. If they were kindly treated, and trusted with some measure of local government, I am sure that the Christian peoples of the Caucasus would never cause the Tsar's ministers any trouble; but if an attempt be made to crush the national spirit, the descendants of the men who fought under Irakli will, at least, show despots how men can die.

APPENDIX.

BIBLIOGRAPHY.

THE standard work on Transcaucasian bibliography is *Miansarov* (M.), Bibliographia Caucasica et Transcaucasica. S. Pbg., 1874—76, 8vo, 804 pp., 4840 refs. It is rather scarce, as the edition was limited to 600 copies. Only one volume has been published, although a second was promised. Most of the works mentioned are in Russian or Armenian, and as far as European publications are concerned, Miansarov is very incomplete. In the following pages I have referred to comparatively few Russian books.

After Miansarov, the following, among many others, may with advantage be consulted :—

Catalogue de la Section des Russica, published by Bibl. imp. publ. de St. Pbg., 1873. 2 vols. 8vo.

Semenov (P.), Geografichsko-statistichskii slovar Rosiiskoi Imperii. Pbg., 1863—1885. 5 vols. 4to.

Stuckenberg (J. Ch.), Versuch eines Quellen-Anzeigers . . . fuer das Studium der Geographie . . . des Russischen Reichs. Pbg., 1849—1852. 2 vols. 8vo.

I am fully conscious of the shortcomings of this essay, and shall be glad to find it extended and corrected by later writers, to whom it may serve as a groundwork.

Works of special interest are marked *.

GEOGRAPHY, TRAVELS, AND MISCELLANEOUS LITERATURE.

*Brosset (M. F.), Description géographique de la Géorgie par

le Tsarévitch Wakhoucht. Texte géorgien ·suivi d'une traduction française. Avec 6 cartes lith. S. Pbg. Acad. Scient., 1842. 4to.

Wakhoucht wrote to the local authorities all over the country, asking each for information about his own district; the present standard work was the result of his inquiries.

ANCIENT GEOGRAPHY.

Cf. *Apollonius Rhodius, Strabo, Plinius, Arrianus, Ptolemæus, C. Rommel's* Caucasiarum Regionum et gentium straboniana descriptio. Lipsiæ, 1804. 8vo.

Luenemann (G. H.), Descriptio Caucasi. Lipsiæ, 1803. 4to.

Carli (Joh. Rinaldi), De expeditione Argonautorum in Colchidem. Venet., 1745. 2 vols. 4to.

Vivien de St. Martin (Louis), Mémoire historique sur la géographie ancienne du Caucase. Paris, 1848.

—— ——, Etude géographique sur le Caucase de Strabon. In Etudes de Géogr. Anc. Paris, 1852.

Preller (E.), Bedeutung des schwarzen Meeres fuer die Handel und Verkehr der alten Welt. Dorpat, 1842. 8vo.

MEDIÆVAL GEOGRAPHY.

Stephanus Byzantinus, Massudi, Abulfeda.

Defrémery, Fragments de géographes et d'historiens arabes et persans inédits, relatifs aux anciens peuples du Caucase. In Nouv. Journ. Asiat., 1849—1851. Paris.

Rubruquis (1253) in Navigantium atque itinerantium bibliotheca, by John Harris, D.D., continued by J. Campbell. 2 vols. in fol. London, 1764. In this collection will be found other records of travel in Georgia.

Barbaro (Josafat), Viaggio alla Tana e nella Persia (1436). In Ramusio's Raccolta di Viaggi. Venetia, 1583.

Contarini (Ambroise), Voyage de Perse (1473). In Bergeron's Collection de Voyages. Paris, 1735.

Sixteenth and Seventeenth Centuries.

Hakluyt (Richd.), The Principall Navigations, Voiages, and Discoveries of the English Nation in . . . the Empire of Russia, the Caspian Sea, Georgia . . . London, 1589. Fol. Also 1600. 3 vols. Fol. New edition, London, 1809—1812. 4to.

Jenkinson (Anthony), Early Voyages and Travels to Russia and Persia, by A. J. and other Englishmen (in reign of Queen Elizabeth). Hakluyt Soc. London, 1886. 2 vols. 8vo.

Zampi (Giuseppe Maria), Relatione della Cholchida. 1620.

Lamberti (Arcangelo), Relatione della Cholchida, hoggi· detta Mengrellia, nella quale si tratta dell' origine, costumi e cose naturali di quei paesi. 2nd edition. Napoli, 1654. 4to.

Olearius (Adam), The Voyages and Travels of the Ambassadors sent by Frederick, Duke of Holstein, to the Great Duke of Muscovy and the King of Persia . . . . in 1633—1639. Translated from the Dutch by J. Davies. London, 1662. 2 vols. Fol.

Dapper (Olfert), Asia . . . . beneffens en volkome Beschryving van geheel Persie, Georgie, Mengrelie en andere Gebuur-gewesten. Amsterdam, 1672. Fol.
—— German edition. Nuernberg. Translated by Beern. 2 vols. Fol. 1681.

Novikov, Drevnaya rossiiskaya biblioteka. S. Pbg., 1788. 8vo. For Travels of Russian Ambassadors to Georgia in Seventeenth Century.

Moreri (Ludvig), Relations nouvelles du Levant, ou Traité de la religion, du gouvernement et des coutumes des Perses, des Arméniens et des Gaures. Lyon, 1671. 12mo.

Bruin (C. de) (Dutch painter) Voyages au Levant. Delft, 1700. Fol.
—— ——, Voyages dans la Moscovie et la Perse. Amsterdam, 1718. 2 vols. Fol. And Paris, 1725. 5 vols. 4to.

Struys (Jean), Voyages en Muscovie, en Tatarie, en Perse, etc. Amsterdam, 1720. 3 vols. 12mo.

Tavernier, Six voyages . . . . en Perse (1663—69). Rouen, 1724.

Chardin (Sir John), The Travels of Sir John Chardin into Persia. London, 1686. Fol. 2 vols.

Tournefort (Pitton de), Rélation d'un Voyage du Levant, contenant l'histoire ancienne et moderne de . . . . l'Arménie, de la Géorgie . . . Paris and Lyon, 1717. 2 vols. 4to. Amsterdam, 1718. English edition, London, 1718. Dutch edition, Amsterdam, 1737.

Evliya (Effendi), Travels in Europe, Asia, and Africa in the Seventeenth Century. Translated from the Turkish by J. von Hammer. London, 1846.

EIGHTEENTH CENTURY.

Lerch (Joh. Jacob), Zweite Reise nach Persien. In Buesching's Magazin. 1776.

Reineggs (Jacob), Beschreibung des Kaukasus. Gotha, 1796—97. 8vo. And some other works. Sketches in Pallas's Nordische Beitraege, etc. A General, Historical, and Topographical Description of Mount Caucasus. Translated by Ch. Wilkinson. London, 1807. (Reineggs was a diplomatic agent of the Russian Court, and induced the Ossets to submit, besides preparing the way for the annexation of Georgia.)

Gueldenstaedt (Joh. Ant.), Geografichskoie i statistichskoie opisanié Gruzii (Geographical and Statistical Description of Georgia). S. Pbg., 1809. 8vo.

—— ——, Reisen nach Georgien und Imerethi, ausg. von J. von Klaproth. Berlin, 1815. 8vo.

—— ——, Beschreibung der Kaukasischen Laender, ausg. von J. von Klaproth. Berlin. 1834. 8vo.

Peyssonnel (French Consul in Smyrna), Traité sur le Commerce de la Mer Noire. Paris, 1787. 2 vols. 8vo.

Memoir of a Map of the Countries comprehended between the Black Sea and the Caspian; with an account of the Caucasian nations, and vocabularies of their languages. London, 1788. 4to.

Howell, Journal of the Passage from India through Armenia, &c.

Wilford (Francis), On Mount Caucasus. In Asiatic Researches. London, 1799.

Potocki (Jean), Voyage dans les steps d'Astrakhan et du Caucase (in 1797) publié par Klaproth. Paris, 1829. 8vo.

Voyages historiques et géographiques dans les pays situés entre la Mer Noire et la Mer Caspienne. Paris, 1798.

Biberstein (Maréchal de), Tableau des provinces situées sur la Côte occidentale de la Mer Caspienne, entre les fleuves Térek et Kour. S. Pbg., 1798. 4to.

Mémoires historiques et géographiques sur les pays situés entre la Mer Noire et la Mer Caspienne. Paris, 1797. 4to.

Natolien, Georgien . . . . in historischer, geographischer politischer Hinsicht. Berlin and Leipzig, 1799. 8vo.

NINETEENTH CENTURY.

Zass (de), Description du Caucase, avec le précis historique et statistique de la Géorgie. S. Pbg., 1804. 8vo.

Langen (Jacob), Opisanié Kavkaza s kratkım ıstorichskim i statistichskim opisaniem Gruzii (Description of the Caucasus, with a short historical and statistical description of Georgia). Translated from the French of J. L. S. Pbg., 1805.

Rommel (V. C.), Die Voelker des Kaukasus. Weimar, 1808.

Lagorio, Extrait du Journal d'un voyage en Mingrélie. In Annales des Voyages. Paris, 1809.

———, Bemerkungen ueber Mingrelien. In Minerva. 1811.

Clarke (E. D.), Voyages en Russie etc., trad. de l'anglais.

Paris, 1812. 2 vols. 8vo. I have not seen the English original.

Morier (John), Journey through Persia. London, 1812. 4to.

——— ———, Second Journey through Persia .... with an account of the embassy of Sir Gore Ouseley. London, 1818. 4to.

Kinneir, Geographical Memoir of the Persian Empire, interspersed with an account of manners and customs. London, 1813. 4to.

———, Journey through Asia Minor, Armenia, &c. London, 1818. 8vo.

Colchis oder Mingrelien. In Hormayr's Archiv. 1813.

Drouville, Voyage en Perse. S. Pbg., 1820. 2 vols. 8vo. With atlas.

Freygang (Wilhelm and Frederica), Lettres sur le Caucase et la Géorgie. Hambourg, 1816. 8vo.

Engelhardt (Moritz von) and *Parrot* (Friedr.), Reise in die Krymm und den Kaukasus. Berlin, 1815. *Parrot* also wrote Reise nach Ararat. Berlin, 1830. Translated by W. D. Cooley, London. n.d. 8vo.

Kotzebue (Moritz von), Reise nach Persien im Jahre 1817.

Johnson (John), A Journey from India to England through Persia, Georgia .... London, 1818. 4to.

Ker-Porter (Sir Robt.), Travels in Georgia, Persia, Armenia, Ancient Babylonia, &c., during the years 1817—1820. London, 1821. 2 vols. 4to.

Lumsden (Thos.), A Journey from Merut in India to London, through Arabia, Persia, Armenia, Georgia .... London, 1822. 8vo.

Gamba (Jacques François), Voyage dans la Russie méridionale, et particulièrement dans les provinces situées au-delà du Caucase, fait depuis 1820 jusqu'en 1824. With an atlas. 2 tom. Paris, 1826. 8vo.

Lyall (Robt.), Travels in Russia, the Crimea, and Georgia. London, 1825. 2 vols. 8vo.

Asiatic Journal. London. Former and Present State of the Road over Mount Caucasus, 1825; Visit to the Caucasian Wall, 1833; The Caucasian Nations, 1837; and other articles.

Bronievskii, Puteshestvié na Kavkazié (Journey in the Caucasus). Moskva, 1825. 2 vols. 8vo.

Henderson, Biblical Researches and Travels in Russia, including . . . . the Passage of the Caucasus. London, 1826. 8vo.

Halen (D. Juan van), Dos años en Rusia. Valencia, 1849. 8vo. Also Mémoires. Paris and Bruxelles, 1827. 2 vols. 8vo.

——, Narrative of D. Juan van Halen's Imprisonment . . . . his Campaign with the Army of the Caucasus. Translated from the Spanish. London, 1827. 2 vols. 8vo. Another edition in 1830.

Klaproth (Julius von), Voyage au Mont Caucase. Paris, 1827. 8vo.

——, Extraits d'une topographie de la Géorgie. Paris, n. d. 8vo. And several other works.

Seristori (Comte), Notes sur les provinces russes au-delà du Caucase. Odessa, 1829.

Vetter (J. C. W.), Meine Reise nach Grusien. Leipzig, 1829.

Rottiers, Itinéraire de Tiflis à Constantinople. Bruxelles, 1829.

Jaeger (B.), Reise von St. Petersburg in die Krim und die Laender des Kaukasus. Leipzig, 1830. 8vo.

Pushkin (A. S.), Puteshestvié v Erzerum (Journey to Erzerum). 1829.

Lermontov (M. Y.), Geroi nashevo vremeni (A Hero of our Times). 1839—40.

Kupfer, Voyage dans les environs du Mont Elbrous. S. Pbg. Acad. Scient., 1830.

Jaeger (B.), Versuch einer Darstellung des natuerlichen Reichthums der russischen Laender jenseit des Kaukasus. Leipzig, 1830. 8vo.

Marigny (E. T. de), Portulan de la Mer Noire. Odessa, 1830.

Guibal (Paul), Industrie et économie des Abazes in Courrier de la Nouvelle Russie. 25 Dec., 1831. Odessa.

Armstrong (T. B.), Travels in Russia and Turkey Itinerary through . . . . Georgia. London, 1831. 8vo.

Budberg (Leonh., Freiherr von), Galerie der neuesten Reisen von Russen durch Russland. S. Pbg., 1832.

L. S. (Cte.) (? Seristori), Notes statistiques sur le littoral de la Mer Noire. Vienne, 1832. 8vo. 22 pp.

Nouv. Annales des Voyages. Paris. Many articles.

Nouv. Journal Asiatique. Paris. Description géographique du Ghouria. 1832. And many other articles.

Annalen der Erdkunde. Blick auf Georgien. 1832. Georgien und seine Umgebung. 1843. And other articles.

Eichwald (Carl Eduard von), Reise auf dem Caspischen Meere und in den Caucasus. Stuttgard, 1834—38. 2 Bde. 8vo. A scientific work.

Mignan, Journal of a Tour through Georgia . . . . Asiatic Society. Bombay, 1834.

Smith (Eli) and *Dwight* (H.), Missionary Researches in Armenia, including a journey . . . . into Georgia. London, 1834. 8vo.

Conolly (Arthur), Journey to the North of India overland. London, 1834. 2 vols. 8vo.

Famin (César), Region caucasienne in Univers pittoresque.

Paris, n. d. 8vo. Caucasien in Weltgemaeldegallerie. Stuttgard, 1835. 8vo.

Hammer (Joseph von), Schwarzes Meer. Wien, 1835.

Evetskii (Orest), Statistichskoé opisanié Kavkaza (Statistical Description of the Caucasus). S. Pbg., 1835.

Obozrenie russkikh vladenii za Kavkazom (Description of the Russian Possessions beyond the Caucasus). S. Pbg., 1836. 4 vols. 8vo. An official publication.

Zubov, Kartina kavkazskavo kraya (Picture of the Caucasian Land). S. Pbg., 1834—35. 4 vols. 8vo.

———, Shest pisem o Gruzii i Kavkazié (Six Letters about Georgia and the Caucasus). Moskva, 1834. 8vo.

Besse, Voyage en Crimée, au Caucase, etc. Paris, 1838. 8vo.

Belanger (Ch.), Voyage aux Indes par . . . . la Géorgie. Paris, 1838. 8vo. With atlas.

Spencer (Edm.), Travels in the Western Caucasus. London, 1838. 2 vols. 8vo.

Fragmens de lettres écrites de Tiflis en Géorgie. In Bibl. univ. de Genève, 1838.

Wilbraham (Capt. Richard), Travels in the Transcaucasian Provinces. London, 1839. 8vo.

**Dubois de Montpéreux* (Frédéric), Voyage autour du Caucase. Paris, 1839—1843. 6 tom. 8vo. A well-written work. I am indebted to Dubois for many bibliographical notes. The same author published an Atlas in five parts in folio, Neuchatel, 1843, to illustrate his book (part 1, Ancient Geography; part 2, Picturesque views; part 3, Architecture; part 4, Archeology; part 5, Geology).

Hamilton (Walter), Researches in Asia Minor, Armenia, &c. London, 1840. 2 vols. 8vo.

Southgate, Horatio. Narrative of a Tour through Armenia. New York, 1840. 12mo.

Samuel (J.), The Remnant found, or the Place of Israel's

Hiding discovered the Result of Personal Investigation during a Missionary Tour in Georgia. London, 1841. 8vo.

Teule (Jul. C.), Pensées . . . . extraites du journal des mes voyages dans . . . . les provinces russes, géorgiennes et tartares du Caucase . . . . Paris, 1842. 2 vols. 8vo.

Hommaire de Hell, Voyage à la Mer Caspienne. Paris, 1845. 3 vols.

√ *Cameron* (Geo. Poulett), Personal Adventures and Excursions in Georgia. London, 1845. 2 vols. 8vo. Cf. United Service Journal. London, 1840—44.

Hagemeister, Zakavkazskie ocherki (Transcaucasian sketches). S. Pbg., 1845. 8vo. Novie (New) do. do. S. Pbg., 1848.

Joselian (Plato), Opisanié Shiomgvimskoi pustini v Gruzii (Description of the Desert of Shiomgvim in Georgia). Tiflis, 1845. 12mo.

—— ——, Puteviya zapiski po Kakhetii (Travel Notes from Kakheti). Tiflis, 1846. 12mo.

Suzannet (Cte. de), Souvenirs de voyage. Les provinces du Caucase. Paris, 1846. 8vo.

√ *Danilevskii* (N.), Kavkaz i evo gorskie zhiteli (The Caucasus and its Mountaineers). Moskva, 1846. 8vo.

—— ——, Der Kaukasus. Physisch-geographisch, statistisch, ethnographisch und strategisch. Leipzig, 1847. 8vo.

Kolenati, Die Ersteigung des Kasbek. In Russ. Archiv. S. Pbg., 1848.

√ *Wagner* (Moritz), Reise nach Kolchis und nach den deutschen Kolonien jenseits des Kaukasus. Leipzig, 1850. 8vo. And Der Kaukasus und das Land der Kosaken. 2te. Ausg. Leipzig, 1850. 2 Bde. 8vo. Translated into English as Travels in Persia, Georgia, and Koordistan. London, 1856. 3 vols. 8vo.

Stackelberg (Count Ernst von), Le Caucase pittoresque, dessiné d'après nature par le Prince G. Gagarine; avec une introduction et un texte explicatif par le Comte E. S. Paris, 1847—59. Fol.

*—— — —, Scènes, paysages, mœurs et costumes du Caucase, dessinés d'après nature par le Prince G. Gagarine, et accompagnés d'un texte par le Comte E. S. Paris, 1850, etc. Fol.

Bodenstedt (Fr.), Tausend und ein Tag im Orient. .Berlin, 1850. 2 vols. 8vo.

Marmier (X.), Du Danube au Caucase. Paris, 1854. 8vo.

Haxthausen (August, Baron v.), Transcaucasia. Translated into English by J. E. Taylor. London, 1854. 8vo.

Golovine (Ivan), The Caucasus. London, 1854. 8vo.

Spencer (Edm.), Turkey, Russia, the Black Sea. London, 1854. 8vo.

Thuemmel (A. R.), Bunte Bilder aus dem Kaukasus. Nuernberg, 1854—55. 2 vols. 8vo.

Borozdin (K. A.), Zakavkazskiya vospominaniya. Mingrelia i Svanetia s 1854 do 1861 g. S. Pbg.

**Dumas* (Alexandre), Le Caucase. Paris, 1859. 4to. A charming book.

Gille (F.), Lettres sur le Caucase   Paris, 1859. 8vo. Cf.

Bocage (V. A. B. du), Rapport fait à la Société de Géographie. Paris, 1860. 8vo.

Chodzko (General), Die neuesten Hoehenmessungen im Kaukasus. In Petermann's Mittheilungen. Gotha, 1859.

—— ——, Die russischen Aufnahmen im Kaukasus. Ibid., 1862.

Moynet, Voyage à la Mer Caspienne et à la Mer Noire. In Charton's "Tour du Monde," 1860. 1er. sém. Paris.

Blanchard, Voyage de Tiflis à Stavropol. In Charton's "Tour du Monde," 1861. 2er. sém. Paris.

Lapinskii (T.), Die Bergvoelker des Kaukasus. Hamburg, 1863. 2 vols. 8vo.

Bianchi (A. de), Viaggi in Armenia e Lazistan. Milano, 1863. 8vo.

Ruepprecht, Barometrische Hoehenbestimmungen im Caucasus, 1860—61. In Mém. de l'Acad. de Sc. S. Pbg., 1864.

Bergé (Adolphe), Voyage en Mingrélie. Paris, 1864. 8vo.

Ussher (John), A Journey from London to Persepolis; including Wanderings in . . . . Georgia. London, 1865. 8vo.

Stebnitzky, Uebersicht der Kaukasischen Statthalterschaft. In Petermann's Mittheil. Gotha, 1865.

Petzholdt, Der Kaukasus. Leipzig, 1866. 2 vols. 8vo.

*Radde (Dr. Gustav, Curator of Caucasian Museum, and corresponding member of R.G.S., London), Bericht ueber die biologisch-geographischen Untersuchungen in den Kaukasus-Laendern. Tiflis, 1866. 4to.

—— ——, Reisen und Forschungen im Kaukasus im 1865. In Petermann's Mittheil. Gotha, 1867. 4to.

—— ——, Vier Vortraege ueber dem Kaukasus. Ibid., 1874.

—— ——, Die drei Langenhochthaeler Imeritiens. Tiflis.

—— ——, Das kaukasische Museum in Tiflis. In Jahresbericht des Vereins fuer Erdkunde. Dresden, 1878.

—— ——, Die Chews'uren und ihr Land. Cassel, 1878. 8vo.

Abich (Hermann), Geologische Beobachtungen auf Reisen in den Gebirgslaendern zwischen Kur und Araxes. Tiflis, 1867. 4to. And other geological works.

Becker (A.), Reise nach dem Kaukasus. Moskau, 1868. 8vo.

Schlotheim, Vier Monate in Grusien. Hermansburg, 1869. 8vo.

Favre, Notes sur quelques glaciers de la chaîne du Caucase. In Bibl. universelle de Génève, 15 Janv., 1869.

Vereschaguine (Basile), Voyage dans les Provinces du Caucase. In Charton's "Tour du Monde." Paris, 1869. 4to.

*Freshfield (Douglas W.), Travels in the Central Caucasus and Bashan. London, 1869. 8vo. Contains an account of the famous ascent of Mkhinvari (Mt. Kazbek). Cf. Mr. Freshfield's Lecture before the Royal Geographical Society, London, March 12, 1888.

Cunynghame (A.), Travels in the Eastern Caucasus. London, 1872. 8vo.

Mounsey (Aug. H.), A Journey through the Caucasus. London, 1872. 8vo.

Lyons (F. A.), Adventures in Lazistan. In Bates's Illustrated Travels. London, 1872.

Dilke (Ashton), An Article on Transcaucasia in the Fortnightly Review. London, 1874.

Grove (F. C.), The Frosty Caucasus. London, 1876. 8vo. (Account of ascent of Elbruz in 1874.)

Bunbury (E. H.), Art. Caucasus in Encyc. Brit. Vol. v. 1876.

Thielmann (Baron Max von), Journey in the Caucasus. Translated by Dr. C. Hemeage. London, 1875. 2 vols. in 1. 8vo.

Ernouf, Le Caucase, le Perse et la Turquie d'Asie. D'après la relation de M. le Baron de Thielmann. Paris, 1876. 8vo.

Schneider, Vorlaeufiger Bericht ueber im Laufe des Sommers 1875 in Transkaukasien ausgefuehrte Reisen. In "Isis." 1876.

Fuchs (P.), Ethnologische Beschreibung der Osseten. In "Ausland." 1876.

Bernoville (Raphael), La Souanétie libre. Illustr. Paris, 1875.

4to. Also Notes d'un voyage au Caucase. In Revue catholique de Bordeaux, Oct. 1883.

Telfer (J. B., Commander R.N.), The Crimea and Transcaucasia. London, 1876. 2 vols. 8vo.

*Bryce (Prof. James), Transcaucasia and Ararat. London, 1877. 8vo.

Bakradse (D.), Das tuerkische Grusien. aus d. Russischen uebers. v. N. v. Seidlitz. In Russ. Revue. 1877.

Call (G. v.), Eisenbahnen im Kaukasus. In Oesterr. Monatsschrift fuer d. Orient. Wien, 1877.

Kohn (A.), Kaukasien und seine Bewohner. In "Grenzboten." 1877.

Reisen im Kaukasus Gebiet. In " Ausland." 1877.

Travels in the Caucasus. In Edinburgh Review. January, 1877.

Cole (G. R. F.), Transcaucasia. In Fraser's Magazine. December, 1877.

Schweizer-Lerchenfeld (A. v.), Lazistan und die Lazen. In Monatsschrift fuer d. Orient. Wien, 1878.

Karsten (K.), Natur- und Kulturbilder aus Transkaukasien. In " Aus allen Welttheilen." 1878.

Smirnow (M.), Aperçu sur l'ethnographie du Caucase. In Revue d'Anthropologie. Paris, 1878.

Kaukasische Skizzen. In Russ. Revue. S. Pbg., 1879.

Art. Georgia in Encyc. Brit. Vol. x. 1879. Only remarkable for its typographical errors.

Vivien de Saint-Martin (Louis), Nouveau dictionnaire de Géographie universelle. Paris, 1879. 4to. Art. *Caucase* and *Géorgie*. Also his Nouv. Annales des Voyages.

Serena (Mme. Carla), Articles in Charton's " Tour du Monde." Paris. 4to. Iméréthi, 1880. Mingrélie, 1881. Kakhétie, 1882. Samourzakan, Abkasie, 1882.

Seidlitz (N. v.), Die Voelker des Kaukasus. In Russische

Revue. 1881. Vide also Petermann's Mittheilungen and Russ. Revue passim.

Reclus (Elisée), Nouvelle Géographie Universelle. Paris, T. vi., 1881. 4to.

— *Morrison* (M. A.), Caucasian Nationalities. In Journal of Royal Asiatic Society. London, 1881.

Wolley (Clive Phillips, formerly British Vice-Consul at Kertch). Sport in the Crimea and Caucasus. London, 1881. 8vo.

—— ——, Savage Svanêtia. 2 vols. London, 1883. 8vo.

Koch (C.), Wanderungen im Oriente. Weimar, 1846—47. 3 vols. 8vo.

—— ——, Die Kaukasische Militaerstrasse. Leipzig, 1851. 8vo.

—— ——, Nachklaenge orientalischer Wanderungen. Erfurt, 1881. 8vo.

Koechlin-Schwartz (A.), Un touriste au Caucase. Paris, 1881. 12mo.

Bayern (Fr.), Contribution à l'archéologie du Caucase. Lyon, 1883.

— *Wanderer* (an English officer), Notes on the Caucasus. London, 1883. 8vo.

Sobolsky (W.), Spuren primitiver Familienordnungen bei den Kaukasischen Bergvoelkern. In Russ. Revue. 1883.

Vladikin, Putevoditel po Kavkazu (Guide to the Caucasus). Moskva, 1885. 2 vols. 8vo.

Chantre (Ernest), Recherches anthropologiques dans le Caucase. Paris and Lyon, 1886. 2 vols. 4to.

Erckert (R. von), Der Kaukasus und seine Voelker. Leipzig, 1887. 8vo. Ethnography.

Kovalevskii, Customs of the Ossetes. In Journ. R. Asiat. Soc., July, 1888. Translated by E. Delmar Morgan, M.R.A.S.

Kavkaz, Spravochnaya kniga. Tiflis, 1888. 12mo.

Weidenbaum (E.), Putevoditel po Kavkazu (Guide to the Caucasus). Tiflis, 1888. An official publication. A good guide on the principle of those of Murray is much wanted, but *Murray's Guide to Russia*, 4th edition, 1888, gives very little information about the Caucasus.

Sbornik Svdenii o Kavkazié, Tiflis, 9 vols., 4to, beginning 1871, contains a mass of interesting and useful information. Vol. I. 1871. Monograph on the *Ossets*, by *Pfaff*. Collection of Georgian, Armenian, and Tatar *proverbs*, &c.— Vol. II. 1872. Statistical and economic condition of the *Ossets*, by *Pfaff*. Serfdom in Georgia at the beginning of the present century by *Kalantarov*. Railway routes to India. —Vol. III. 1874. Exhaustive Treatise on *Viniculture* in the Caucasus.—Vol. IV. and V. 1878—79. Statistics. —Vol. VI. 1880. *Tiflis* according to the census of March 25, 1876. Also contains a brief historical account of the city.—Vol. VII. 1880. And Vols. VIII. and IX. 1885. Statistics.

Sbornik materialov dlya opisaniya myestnostei i plemen Kavkaza. The sixth volume was published in Tiflis this year.

For ARCHEOLOGY vide—

Akti of the *Kavkazskaya Arkhéografichskaya Kommissiya* of Tiflis, from 1866. In fol. Also the *Zapiski* and *Izvestiya* of the *Obshchestvo Lyubitelei Kavkazskoi Arkhéologii* of Tiflis. Former, from 1875, in fol.; latter, from 1877, in 8vo.

The BEST MAP is that of the General Staff. Five versts to the inch.

HISTORY.

GENERAL.

Brosset (M. F.), Histoire de la Géorgie (two volumes of Georgian text, and six volumes of French translation and notes). S. Pbg. (Acad. Scient.), 1849—58. 4to. M. Brosset has written a great many books and articles on Georgian history, published by the Imperial Academy of Sciences in S. Pbg.; some of them may still be purchased.

Cf. Bibliographie analytique des ouvrages de M. Marie-Félicité Brosset .... par M. Laurent Brosset. S. Pbg., 1887.

Joselian (Plato), Istoriya gruzinskoi tserkvi. S. Pbg., 1843. Translated into English under the title of "A Short History of the Georgian Church," translated from the Russian by the Rev. S. C. Malan. London, 1866. 8vo.

—— ——, Razlichniya naimenovaniya Gruzin (On the various Appellations of the Georgians). Tiflis, 1846. 12mo.

—— ——, Istorichskii vzglad na sostoyanie drevnei Gruzii (Historical glance at the condition of ancient Georgia). In Zhurnal Ministerstva narodn. Prosv. S. Pbg., 1843. Cf. also his periodical Zakavkazskii Vestnik from 1845. Tiflis.

Baratov (Prince Sulkhan), Istoriya Gruzii. S. Pbg., 1865, &c. 8vo.

David (Tsarevich of Georgia), Kratkaya istoriya o Gruzii. S. Pbg., 1805. 12mo.

Barataiev, Numizmatichskie fakti Gruzinskavo tsarstva (Georgian numismatics). S. Pbg., 1844. 8vo.

Villeneuve (de), La Géorgie. Paris, 1870. 8vo.

Breitenbauch (Georg Aug. von), Geschichte der Staaten von Georgien. Memmingen, 1788. Thin 8vo.

Reineggs (Jacob), Kurzer Auszug der Geschichte von Georgien. Published in P. S. Pallas's Neue Nordische Beitraege, III. Bd., S. Pbg., 1781. 8vo.

*Evgeny (Bolkovitinov, Metropolitan of Kiev), Georgien, oder historisches Gemaelde von Grusien, aus dem Russischen uebers. von F. Schmidt. Riga, 1804. 8vo. A capital little book.

Malcolm (Sir John), History of Persia. 2nd edition. London 1829. 8vo.

Fraser, An Historical and Descriptive Account of Persia. Edinburgh, 1834. 12mo.

Kazem-Beg, Derbend Nàmeh, or the History of Derbend. Translated from the Turkish (into English). S. Pbg., 1851. 4to.

EARLY HISTORY.

Ditmar (T. J.), Von den kaukasischen Voelkern der mythischen Zeit. Berlin, 1789. 8vo.

Ritter (Carl), Die Vorhalle Europaeischer Voelkergeschichten vor Herodotus, um den Kaukasus und an den Gestaden des Pontus, eine Abhandlung zur Alterthumskunde. Berlin, 1820. 8vo. The copy in the British Museum is lettered "Ritter's Wahnsinn," and we must own that we think the book more interesting than instructive.

Neumann (Carl), Die Hellenen im Skythenlande. Berlin, 1855. 8vo.

Shea (D.), Mīr Khwānd. History of the Early Kings of Persia from Kaiomars to . . . . Alexander the Great. London. Oriental Translation Fund. 1832. 8vo.

Procopius, De bello persico . . . . De bello gothico. Continued down to 560 A.D. by *Agathias*.

Constantinus Porphyrius (X. cent. A.D.), De administrando imperio.

Boyer, De muro caucasico. In vol. i. of Comment. de l'Acad. de Sciences. S. Pbg.

Polybius, De bello persico. Lib. i., cap. xii. et passim.

Ruffinus, Historia ecclesiastica. Lib. i., cap. x. Conversion of Georgia.

Saint-Martin (Jean Antoine), Mémoires historiques et géographiques sur l'Arménie. 2 tom. Paris, 1818 and 1819. 8vo.

Ashik (Anton), Bosforskoye Tsarstvo s yevo paleografichskimi i nadgrobnimi pamyatnikami, raspisnimi vasami, planami, kartami i vidami (The Kingdom of the Bosphorus, with its paleographic and monumental remains, inscribed vases, plans, maps, and views). Odessa, 1848—49. Three parts. 4to.

Neumann (C. F.), Elisha Vartabed. The History of Vartan, and of the battles of the Armenians. 1830. 8vo. And Vahram's Chronicle of the Armenian Kingdom in Cilicia. 1831. 8vo. Published by Oriental Translation Fund. London.

D'Ohsson (Chév.), Des peuples du Caucase au Xe. siècle. Paris, 1828.

Lebeau (Charles), Histoire du Bas Empire. Corrigée et augm. par M. de Saint-Martin et continuée par M. Brosset jeune. 20 tom. Paris, 1824—36. 8vo.

Vivien de Saint-Martin (Louis), Recherches sur les populations primitives et les plus anciennes traditions du Caucase. Paris, 1847. 8vo.

Stritter (J. G.), Memoriæ populorum olim ad Danubium, Pontum Euxinum, Paludem Mæotidem, Caucasum, Mare Caspium, et inde magis ad Septentriones, incolentium, e scriptoribus Historiæ Byzantinæ erutæ et digestæ. Petropoli, 1771—79. 4 vols. 4to. (Vol. iv. refers to Georgian History.)

Modern History.

Klaproth (J. von), Aperçu des entreprises des Mongols en Géorgie . . . . dans le XIII. siècle. Paris, 1833. 8vo.

Comte L. S. (? Seristori), Memoria sulle colonie del Mar Nero nei secoli di mezzo. 26 pp. 8vo. (n. d.) An account of the Genoese trading colonies.

Dorn (B.), Beitraege zur Geschichte der Kaukasischen Laender und Voelker, aus morgenlaendischen Quellen. Esp. III. Bd. (Geschichte der Georgier), which contains a work by a Mahometan writer named Iskender Munshi, and a History of the Szafid Dynasty; it deals with the period 1540—1663. Acad. Scient. S. Pbg., 1844. 4to.

*Perepiska na inostrannikh yazikakh gruzinskikh tsarei s rosiiskimi gosudaryami ot 1639 g. do 1770 g. (Correspondence in foreign languages between the Kings of Georgia and the Sovereigns of Russia from 1639 to 1770.) Acad. Scient. S. Pbg., 1861. 4to.

Hanway (Jonas), The Revolutions of Persia during the present century (being the second volume of the Historical Account of the British trade over the Caspian). 2nd edition. London, 1754. 4to.

Der allerneueste Staat von Casan . . . . Georgien und vieler andern dem Czaren, Sultan und Schach . . . . unterthanen Tartarn Landschaften . . . . Nuernberg, 1724. 8vo.

Van der Quelle (Philander—pseudonym), Leben und Thaten des persischen Monarchen Schach Nadyr. Leipzig, 1738. 8vo.

Peyssonnel (French Consul in Smyrna), Histoire des Troubles dans la Géorgie. (? Paris, 1754.) 8vo. Translated into German, also into English as a continuation of Hanway's History. London, 1756. 4to.

Ouosk' Herdjan (Jean), Mémoire pour servir à l'histoire des événemens qui ont eu lieu en Arménie et en Géorgie à la fin du XVIIIe. siècle et au commencement du XIXe. Trad. de l'arménien par J. Klaproth. Paris, 1818. 8vo.

Cirbied (J.), Histoire arménienne; details sur les changements politiques en Géorgie et en Arménie dans les premières années du XIXe. siècle. (? Paris, 1818.) 8vo

Rottiers (Col.), Notice biographique sur Marie, dernière reine de Géorgie. Journal Asiatique. Tom. 10. Paris, 1827.

*Zubov, Podvigi russkikh voisk v stranakh kavkazskikh v 1810—34 (The Exploits of the Russian Army in the Caucasian Countries from 1810 to 1834). S. Pbg., 1835—36. Ten vols. 8vo. With portraits and plans.

——, Kartina voini s Persieiu (A Picture of the War with Persia). S. Pbg., 1834. 8vo.

Fonton (Félix de), La Russie dans l'Asie Mineure. Histoire de la campagne du Maréchal Paskewitch. Paris, 1831. 8vo. With atlas.

Urquhart (David), Progress and Present Position of Russia in the East. London, 1836. 8vo. And second edition " continued to the present time." London, 1854. 8vo.

Hommaire de Hell, Situation des Russes dans le Caucase. Paris, 1844. 8vo.

Holland (Thomas Erskine), Lecture on the Treaty Relations of Russia and Turkey from 1774—1853. London and Oxford, 1877. 8vo.

Haxthausen (August, Baron von), The Tribes of the Caucasus, with an account of Shamyl. Translated by J. E. Taylor. London, 1855. 12mo.

Moser (L.), Der Kaukasus, seine Voelkerschaften .... nebst einer Charakteristik Schamils. Wien, 1854. 8vo.

Our Dangerous Neighbour over the Way, and Two Questions upon the Caucasus. London, 1854. 8vo.

*Bodenstedt (Friedrich Martin), Die Voelker des Kaukasus und ihre Freiheitskaempfe gegen die Russen. 2 Bde. 2te. Ausg. Berlin, 1855. 8vo.

Wagner (Dr. Friedr.), Schamyl als Feldherr, Sultan und Prophet. Leipzig, 1854. 8vo. English translation by L. Wraxall. London, 1856. 8vo.

Douhaire (P.), Les Russes au Caucase. Prise de Schamyl. Paris, 1859. 8vo.

*Dubrovin, Istoriya voini i vladichestva russkikh na Kavkazié (History of the War and Supremacy of the Russians in the Caucasus). 3 vols. S. Pbg., 1871. The first volume is introductory, and contains an excellent ethnographical account of the country.

Baumgarten (G.), Sechzig Jahre des kaukasischen Krieges. Nach russischen Originalen .... Leipzig, 1861. 8vo.

Dulaurier, La Russie dans le Caucase. In Revue des Deux Mondes. Paris, 1865—66.

Boys (A. du), Le Caucase depuis Shamyl. In Le Contemporain. Paris, 25 Août, 1876.

The following PERIODICAL PUBLICATIONS should also be consulted :—

The official newspaper *Kavkaz*. 1844—88. Tiflis.

✓ *Kavkazskii Sbornik.* 1876—86. 10 vols. 8vo. Tiflis. A series of articles chiefly referring to Russian military exploits in the Caucasus during the present century.

For GEORGIAN JURISPRUDENCE, cf.—

Sbornik zakonov gruzinskavo tsarya Vakhtanga VI. (Collection of the laws of the Georgian King Vakhtanga VI.), izd. A. S. *Frenkelya*, pod redak. *D. Z. Bakradze*. Tiflis, 1887. *Bagaturov* (S. J.), Lichniya i pozemelniya prava v drevnei Gruzii (Personal and Agrarian Laws in Ancient Georgia). Tiflis, 1886. *Dareste*, An Art. in Journ. des Savants. Paris, 1887. *Kovalevskii*, Arts. in Vestnik Yevropi.

LANGUAGE AND LITERATURE.

GEORGIAN GRAMMARS AND DICTIONARIES—COMPARATIVE PHILOLOGY.

Alphabetum Ibericum sive Georgianum. Romæ, 1629. 8vo.

Paolini (Stefano), Dittionario Giorgiano e Italiano, composto da S. P. con l'aiuto del M. R. P. D. Niceforo Irbachi Giorgiano. Roma (Propag.), 1629. 4to.

Maggi (Francesco Maria), Syntagmatωn linguarum Orientalium quæ in Georgiæ regionibus audiuntur. Romæ, 1643. Fol. And 1670. Fol.

Hyde (Thomas, D.D.), Historia religionis veterum Persarum .... Oxonii, 1700. 4to. And 1760. 4to. Contains Georgian alphabet.

Tlukaanti (David), Dottrina Cristiana per uso delle missioni della Giorgia, tradotta dalla lingua italiana in lingua civile giorgiana. Roma, 1741. 8vo. And 1800. 8vo.

Vocabularium Catherinæ. Nos. 108, 109, 110, &c. S. Pbg.

Varlaamov, Kratkaya gruzinskaya grammatika. S. Pbg., 1802.

Hervas, Vocabolario poliglota, p. 164, &c. Madrid.

Witsen, Nord en Oost Tartarye II., 506, 526.

Firalov, Samouchitel, soderzhashchii v sebé Grammatiku, Razgovori, Nravoucheniya i Lexikon, na Rossiiskom i Gruzinskom yazikakh (Grammar, Dialogues, Moral Precepts, and Dictionary in Russian and Georgian). S. Pbg., 1820. 8vo.

Vater (J. S.), Vergleichungstafeln der Europaeischen Stamm-Sprachen .... Grusinische Grammatik, nach Maggio, Ghai und Firalow .... Halle, 1822. 8vo.

Klaproth (H. J. v.), Kaukasische Sprachen. Halle and Berlin, 1814. 8vo.

—— ——, Vocabulaire et grammaire de la langue géorgienne. Paris (Soc. Asiat.), 1827. 8vo.
Sur la langue Géorgienne. In Journal Asiat. Paris, 1827.

Brosset (M. F.), L'Art libéral ou grammaire géorgienne. Paris, 1830. 8vo.

—— ——, Éléments de la langue géorgienne. Paris, 1837. 8vo.

Soulkhanoff (A.), Vocabulaire méthodique géorgien-français-russe. S. Pbg, 1839. 8vo.

*Chubinov (David), Gruzinsko-russo-frantsuzkii slovar. Dictionnaire géorgien-français-russe avec un abrégé de la grammaire géorgienne par M. Brosset. S. Pbg., 1840. 4to.

—— ——, Kratkaya gruzinskaya grammatika. S. Pbg., 1855. 8vo.

—— ——, Russko-gruzinskii slovar. Vnov sostavlenii po noveishim russkim slovaryam. S. Pbg., 1886. 8vo.

Bopp, Kaukasische Glieder des Indo-Europaeischen Sprachstamms. Berlin, 1847.

Mueller (F. C. J.), Zur Conjugation des georgischens Verbums. Wien, 1869. 8vo.

✓ *Schiefner* (Prof.), Report on the languages of the Caucasus. In Transactions of Philological Society. London, 1877.

Gatteyrias (J. A.), Etudes linguistiques sur les langues de la famille géorgienne. In Revue de linguistique. Paris, Juillet, 1881.

Tsagareli (Prof.), Georgische Inschrift aus Jerusalem. In Zeitschrift des Palestina-Vereins. 1881.

* ———— ————, Examen de la littérature relative à la grammaire géorgienne. S. Pbg., 1873.

Peacock (D. R.), Original Vocabularies of Five West Caucasian Languages (Georgian, Mingrelian, Lazian, Svanetian, and Apkhazian). Journal of Royal Asiatic Society, 1877, pp. 145—156.

Osset, Mingrelian, Abkhazian, Svanetian, and Lazian Languages.

Sjögren (A. J.), Ossetische Sprachlehre (also published in Russian). S. Pbg. (Acad. Scient.), 1844. 4to.

———— ————, Ossetische Studien. S. Pbg. (Acad. Scient.), 1848. 4to.

Schiefner (A.), Ossetinskie texti (Osset texts). S. Pbg. (Acad. Scient.), 1868. 8vo.

———— ————, Versuch ueber die Thusch-Sprache. S. Pbg. (Acad. Scient.), 1856. 4to. And other works.

Mueller (F. C. J.), Ueber die Stellung des Ossetischen. Wien, 1861. 8vo.

———— ————, Beitraege zur Lautlehre des Ossetischen. Wien, 1863. 8vo.

Miller (Vsyevolod, Professor at Moscow), Ossetinskie etyudi.

Bartolomaei (Lieut.-Gen.), Lushnu Anban. Svanetskaya Azbuka (Svanetian Primer with Georgian and Russian translation. Includes a large vocabulary, Lord's Prayer, colloquial phrases, &c.). Tiflis, 1864. 4to. 147 pp.

Klaproth (J. de), Détails sur le dialecte géorgien usité en Mingrélie. In Journ. Asiat. Paris, 1829.

Rosen, Sprache der Lazen. Berlin, 1840.
——, Abhandlungen ueber das Mingrelische. Berlin 1840.
——, Ueber das Suanische und Abchasische. Berlin, 1845.

GEORGIAN LITERATURE.—Translations and criticisms.

*Brosset, Articles, Lectures, &c , published by Acad. Scient. S. Pbg. in their periodical and other publications.

*Leist (Arthur), Georgische Dichter. Leipzig, 1887. 12mo. A collection of modern lyrics translated into German verse.
—— ——, Georgien, Natur, Sitten u. Bewohner. Leipzig, 1885. (Last chapter contains a short history of Georgian literature, which I freely used in writing the present work.)

*Evgeny (Bolkovitinov), Georgien, oder historisches Gemaelde von Grusien, aus dem Russischen uebers. von F. Schmidt. Riga, 1804. 8vo.

Alter (Franz C), Ueber georgianische Litteratur. Wien, 1798. 8vo.

*Gulak (N. I.), O barsovoi kozhé Rustaveli. (Two lectures in Russian on Rustaveli's " Man in the Panther's Skin.") Tiflis, 1884. 8vo.

État actuel de la littérature Géorgienne. In Nouv. Journ. Asiat. Vol. I., p. 434.

Gabriel (Bishop of Imereti), Sermons, &c. Translated from the Georgian by S. C. Malan, Vicar of Broadwindsor. London, 1867. 8vo.

Orbeliani (Prince Sulkhan), Kniga mudrosti i lzhi. (A Russian translation of a collection of Georgian fables and folk tales of the seventeenth and eighteenth centuries.) Perevod i obyasneniya A. Tsagareli. S. Pbg. (Acad. Scient.), 1878. 8vo.

Bebur B Gruzinskiya narodniya skazki. S. Pbg., 1884. 8vo. (A collection of folk tales, &c., chiefly from Guri.)

Mueller (W.), Prometheische Sagen im Kaukasus. In Russische Revue. 1883.

Bleçki (R. v.), Das Schloss der Tamara. Eine kaukasische Sage. S. Pbg., 1852. 8vo.

Tsagareli (Prof.), Svedeniya o pamyatnikakh gruzinskoi pismennosti (Information concerning the monuments of Georgian literature). S. Pbg., 1887. 8vo.

Morfill (W. R.), An Article on Georgian Literature in "The Academy," July 21, 1888.

Mr. Morfill has catalogued the Georgian Library presented to the Indian Institute at Oxford by the Rev. S. C. Malan, with whom he shares the honour of being the only Georgian scholar in England, and he will shortly publish a History of Russia, a chapter of which will be devoted to Georgia.

STATISTICS.

All the following figures are from official papers, and they refer to the year 1886. They must not be too implicitly believed:—

A. Statistics of Population.

	Area in sq. km.	Total population.
Government of Tiflis	40,473	735,000
,, Kutais	35,000	814,000

Population of the chief towns in Georgia:—

Government of Tiflis.		Government of Kutais.	
Akhaltzikhe	13,265	Batum	11,878
Akhalkalaki	4,303	Kutais	20,227
Gori	5,386	Poti	4,785
Dushet	2,041	Sukhum	1,279
Signakh	10,069		
Telav	8,014		
Tiflis	104,024		

It will be seen that the *urban population is very small.*

B. Trade and Agriculture (1886).

Total trade of Transcaucasia (value in roubles at, say 22*d.* per rouble):—

Exports.	Imports.	Total.
27,812,402	11,452,145	39,264,547 Rbl.

Trade of the interior of Russia and Transcaucasia with Persia:—

Exports.	Imports.	Total.
6,128,933	10,256,056	16,384,989 Rbl.

Transit trade through Transcaucasia:—

From Asia to Europe.	From Europe to Asia.	Total
1,017,607	95,614	1,113,221

Traffic returns of Transcaucasian Railway.

Total weight of goods carried, 58,000,000 puds (Ton = 62 puds).

To Batum and Poti, for export, 32,000,000 puds.

   viz. 15,000,000 pd. petroleum and its products.
       9,000,000 pd. grain.
       8,000,000 pd. miscellaneous goods.

Goods imported from abroad and despatched from Batum and Poti by railway, 5,000,000 pd.

Bread stuffs produced in Transcaucasia:—

Wheat	50,000,000 puds.
Barley	30,000,000 ,,
Maize	20,000,000 ,,
Millet	9,000,000 ,,
Rice	5,000,000 ,,
Oats	350,000 ,,
Potatoes	4,000,000 ,,
Total	118,350,000 puds.

Wine.—The total annual production of wine in Transcaucasia was about 25,000,000 gallons, of which about 15,000,000 gallons in the government of Kutais.

The Transcaucasian Rwy. carried a weight of 247,000

puds from stations in the government of Kutais; 173,000 puds from stations in the government of Tiflis.

(As there is no railway to Kakheti, the wine from that district comes to the capital by road, in carts.)

Two hundred thousand puds were sent to Batum, presumably for export (chiefly to France, where it is "manipulated" and sold as Burgundy).

Sundry goods despatched by Transcaucasian Railway.

	From stations in the govt. of Kutais. Puds.	From stations in the govt. of Tiflis. Puds.
Manganese ore	3,800,000 {chiefly to Great Britain}	—
Timber	536,000	817,000
Dried raisins	—	116,000
Palm wood	23,000	
Walnut wood	20,000	12,000
Walnuts	6,000	36,000
Tobacco	64,000	31,000
Silk and cocoons.	—	1,500
Wool .	—	195,000
Fruits .	70,000	110,000
Raw hides	8,000	36,000
Manufactured hides	21,000	45,000

C. Education (1886).

No. of Schools.

	Higher gymnasia, &c.	Lower municipal	Private schools.	Elementary schools.	Total No. of schools.
Government of Tiflis	17	16	35	339	407
„ Kutais	5	9	7	459	480

No. of Pupils.

	Boys.	Girls	Total.	For every 10,000 inhabitants there are—	
				Schools.	Pupils.
Government of Tiflis .	16,282	6,727	23,009	5·03	284
,, Kutais .	19,234	1,662	20,896	5·90	257

SPECIMENS OF GEORGIAN VOCAL MUSIC.

1.—THE RIVER ARAGVA.

2.—THE SINGER.

GEORGIAN VOCAL MUSIC.

3.—AVTANDIL'S SONG.

4.—DRINKING SONG (p. 88).

LONDON ·
PRINTED BY GILBERT AND RIVINGTON LIMITED,
ST. JOHN'S HOUSE CLERKENWELL ROAD.

A Catalogue of American and Foreign Books Published or Imported by MESSRS. SAMPSON LOW & CO. *can be had on application.*

St. Dunstan's House, Fetter Lane, Fleet Street, London,
September, 1888.

A Selection from the List of Books
PUBLISHED BY
SAMPSON LOW, MARSTON, SEARLE, & RIVINGTON,
LIMITED.

ALPHABETICAL LIST.

*A*BBOTT *(C. C.) Poaetquissings Chronicle.* 10s. 6d.

—— *Waste Land Wanderings.* Crown 8vo, 7s. 6d.

Abney (W. de W.) and Cunningham. Pioneers of the Alps. With photogravure portraits of guides. Imp. 8vo, gilt top, 21s.

Adam (G. Mercer) and Wetherald. An Algonquin Maiden. Crown 8vo, 5s.

Adams (C. K.) Manual of Historical Literature. Cr. 8vo, 12s. 6d.

Agassiz (A.) Three Cruises of the Blake. Illustrated. 2 vols., 8vo, 42s.

Alcott. Works of the late Miss Louisa May Alcott :
  Eight Cousins. Illustrated, 2s.; cloth gilt, 3s. 6d.
  Jack and Jill. Illustrated, 2s.; cloth gilt, 3s. 6d.
  Jo's Boys. 5s.
  Jimmy's Cruise in the Pinafore, &c. Illustrated, cloth, 2s.; gilt edges, 3s. 6d.
  Little Men. Double vol., 2s.; cloth, gilt edges, 3s. 6d.
  Little Women. 1s. } 1 vol., cloth, 2s. ; larger ed., gilt
  Little Women Wedded. 1s. } edges, 3s. 6d.
  Old-fashioned Girl. 2s.; cloth, gilt edges, 3s. 6d.
  Rose in Bloom. 2s.; cloth gilt, 3s. 6d.
  Silver Pitchers. Cloth, gilt edges, 3s. 6d.
  Under the Lilacs. Illustrated, 2s ; cloth gilt, 5s.
  Work : a Story of Experience 1s. } 1 vol., cloth, gilt
  —— Its Sequel, "Beginning Again." 1s. } edges, 3s. 6d.

Alden (W. L.) Adventures of Jimmy Brown, written by himself. Illustrated. Small crown 8vo, cloth, 2s.

Aldrich (T. B.) Friar Jerome's Beautiful Book, &c. 3s. 6d.

Alford (Lady Marian) Needlework as Art. With over 100 Woodcuts, Photogravures, &c. Royal 8vo, 21s. ; large paper, 84s.

Amateur Angler's Days in Dove Dale : Three Weeks' Holiday in 1884. By E. M. 1s. 6d. ; boards, 1s. ; large paper, 5s.

Andersen. Fairy Tales. An entirely new Translation. With over 500 Illustrations by Scandinavian Artists. Small 4to, 6s.

Anderson (W.) Pictorial Arts of Japan. With 80 full-page and other Plates, 16 of them in Colours. Large imp. 4to, £8 8s. (in four folio parts, £2 2s. each); Artists' Proofs, £12 12s.

Angler's Strange Experiences (An). By COTSWOLD ISYS. With numerous Illustrations, 4to, 5s. New Edition, 3s. 6d.

Angling. See Amateur, "British," "Cutcliffe," "Fennell," "Halford," "Hamilton," "Martin," "Orvis," "Pennell," "Pritt," "Senior," "Stevens," "Theakston," "Walton," "Wells," and "Willis-Bund."

Annals of the Life of Shakespeare, from the most recent authorities. Fancy boards, 2s.

Annesley (C.) Standard Opera Glass. Detailed Plots of 80 Operas. Small 8vo, sewed, 1s. 6d.

Antipodean Notes, collected on a Nine Months' Tour round the World. By Wanderer, Author of "Fair Diana." Crown 8vo, 7s. 6d.

Appleton. European Guide. 2 Parts, 8vo, 10s. each.

Armytage (Hon. Mrs.) Wars of Victoria's Reign. 5s.

Art Education. See "Biographies," "D'Anvers," "Illustrated Text Books," "Mollett's Dictionary."

Artistic Japan. Illustrated with Coloured Plates. Monthly. Royal 4to, 2s.

Attwell (Prof.) The Italian Masters. Crown 8vo, 3s. 6d.

Audsley (G. A.) Handbook of the Organ. Top edge gilt, 42s.; large paper, 84s.

—— *Ornamental Arts of Japan.* 90 Plates, 74 in Colours and Gold, with General and Descriptive Text. 2 vols., folio, £15 15s.; in specially designed leather, £23 2s

—— *The Art of Chromo-Lithography.* Coloured Plates and Text. Folio, 63s.

—— *and Tomkinson. Ivory and Wood Carvings of Japan.* 84s. Artists' proofs (100), 168s.

Auerbach (B.) Brigitta. (B. Tauchnitz Collection.) 2s.

—— *On the Heights.* 3 vols., 6s.

—— *Spinoza.* 2 vols., 18mo, 4s.

BADDELEY (S.) Tchay and Chianti. Small 8vo, 5s.

Baldwin (James) Story of Siegfried. 6s

—— *Story of the Golden Age.* Illustrated by HOWARD PYLE. Crown 8vo, 6s.

Baldwin (James) Story of Roland. Crown 8vo, 6s.

Bamford (A. J.) Turbans and Tails. Sketches in the Unromantic East. Crown 8vo, 7s. 6d.

Barlow (Alfred) Weaving by Hand and by Power. With several hundred Illustrations. Third Edition, royal 8vo. £1 5s.

Barlow (P. W.) Kaipara, Experiences of a Settler in N. New Zealand. Illust., c own 8vo, 6s.

Barrow (J.) Mountain Ascents in Cumberland and Westmoreland. Crown 8vo, 7s. 6d.; new edition, 5s.

Bassett (F. S.) Legends and Superstitions of the Sea. 7s. 6d.

THE BAYARD SERIES.

Edited by the late J. HAIN FRISWELL.

Comprising Pleasure Books of Literature produced in the Choicest Style.

"We can hardly imagine better books for boys to read or for men to ponder over."—*Times.*

Price 2s 6d *each Volume, complete in itself, flexible cloth extra, gilt edges, with silk Headbands and Registers.*

The Story of the Chevalier Bayard.	Lord Chesterfield's Letters, Sentences, and Maxims. With Essay by Sainte-Beuve.
Joinville's St. Louis of France.	
The Essays of Abraham Cowley.	
Abdallah. By Edouard Laboullaye.	The King and the Commons. Cavalier and Puritan Songs.
Napoleon, Table-Talk and Opinions.	
Words of Wellington.	Vathek. By William Beckford.
Johnson's Rasselas. With Notes.	Essays in Mosaic. By Ballantyne.
Hazlitt's Round Table.	My Uncle Toby; his Story and his Friends. By P. Fitzgerald.
The Religio Medici, Hydriotaphia, &c. By Sir Thomas Browne, Knt.	
	Reflections of Rochefoucauld.
Coleridge's Christabel, &c. With Preface by Algernon C. Swinburne.	Socrates: Memoirs for English Readers from Xenophon's Memorabilia. By Edw. Levien.
Ballad Poetry of the Affections. By Robert Buchanan.	
	Prince Albert's Golden Precepts.

A *Case containing* 12 *Volumes, price* 31s 6d ; *or the Case separately, price* 3s. 6d.

Baynes (Canon) Hymns and other Verses. Crown 8vo, sewed, 1s.; cloth, 1s. 6d.

Beaugrand (C.) Walks Abroad of Two Young Naturalists. By D. SHARP. Illust., 8vo, 7s. 6d.

Beecher (H. W.) Authentic Biography, and Diary. [*Preparing*

Behnke and Browne. Child's Voice: its Treatment with regard to After Development. Small 8vo, 3s. 6d.

Beyschlag. Female Costume Figures of various Centuries. 12 reproductions of pastel designs in portfolio, imperial. 21s.

Bickersteth (Bishop E. H.) Clergyman in his Home. 1s.

—— —— *Evangelical Churchmanship.* 1s.

Bickersteth (Bishop E. H.) From Year to Year: Original
Poetical Pieces. Small post 8vo, 3s. 6d.; roan, 6s. and 5s.; calf or morocco, 10s. 6d.

—— *The Master's Home-Call.* 20th Thous. 32mo, cloth gilt, 1s.

—— *The Master's Will.* A Funeral Sermon preached on the Death of Mrs. S. Gurney Buxton. Sewn, 6d.; cloth gilt, 1s.

—— *The Reef, and other Parables.* Crown 8vo, 2s. 6d.

—— *Shadow of the Rock.* Select Religious Poetry. 2s. 6d.

—— *The Shadowed Home and the Light Beyond.* 5s.

Bigelow (John) France and the Confederate Navy. An International Episode. 7s. 6d.

Biographies of the Great Artists (Illustrated). Crown 8vo, emblematical binding, 3s. 6d. per volume, except where the price is given.

Claude le Lorrain, by Owen J. Dullea.
Correggio, by M. E. Heaton. 2s. 6d.
Della Robbia and Cellini. 2s. 6d.
Albrecht Durer, by R. F. Heath.
Figure Painters of Holland.
Fra Angelico, Masaccio, and Botticelli.
Fra Bartolommeo, Albertinelli, and Andrea del Sarto.
Gainsborough and Constable.
Ghiberti and Donatello. 2s. 6d.
Giotto, by Harry Quilter.
Hans Holbein, by Joseph Cundall.
Hogarth, by Austin Dobson.
Landseer, by F. G. Stevens.
Lawrence and Romney, by Lord Ronald Gower. 2s. 6d.
Leonardo da Vinci.
Little Masters of Germany, by W. B. Scott.
Mantegna and Francia.
Meissonier, by J. W. Mollett. 2s. 6d.
Michelangelo Buonarotti, by Clément.
Murillo, by Ellen E. Minor. 2s. 6d.
Overbeck, by J. B. Atkinson.
Raphael, by N. D'Anvers.
Rembrandt, by J. W. Mollett.
Reynolds, by F. S. Pulling.
Rubens, by C. W. Kett.
Tintoretto, by W. R. Osler.
Titian, by R. F. Heath.
Turner, by Cosmo Monkhouse.
Vandyck and Hals, by P. R. Head.
Velasquez, by E. Stowe.
Vernet and Delaroche, by J. Rees.
Watteau, by J. W. Mollett. 2s. 6d.
Wilkie, by J. W. Mollett.

Bird (F. J.) American Practical Dyer's Companion. 8vo, 42s.

—— *(H. E.) Chess Practice.* 8vo, 2s. 6d.

Black (Robert) Horse Racing in France: a History. 8vo, 14s.

Black (Wm.) Novels. See "Low's Standard Library."

—— *Strange Adventures of a House-Boat.* 3 vols., 31s. 6d.

—— *In Far Lochaber.* 3 vols., crown 8vo., 31s. 6d.

Blackburn (Charles F.) Hints on Catalogue Titles and Index Entries, with a Vocabulary of Terms and Abbreviations, chiefly from Foreign Catalogues. Royal 8vo, 14s.

Blackburn (Henry) Breton Folk. With 171 Illust. by RANDOLPH CALDECOTT. Imperial 8vo, gilt edges, 21s.; plainer binding, 10s. 6d.

—— *Pyrenees.* Illustrated by GUSTAVE DORÉ, corrected to 1881. Crown 8vo, 7s. 6d. See also CALDECOTT.

Blackmore (R. D.) Lorna Doone. Édition de luxe. Crown 4to, very numerous Illustrations, cloth, gilt edges, 31*s.* 6*d.*; parchment, uncut, top gilt, 35*s.*; new issue, plainer, 21*s.*; small post 8vo, 6*s.*

—— *Novels.* See "Low's Standard Library."

—— *Springhaven.* Illust. by PARSONS and BARNARD. Sq. 8vo, 12*s.*

Blaikie (William) How to get Strong and how to Stay so. Rational, Physical, Gymnastic, &c., Exercises. Illust., sm post 8vo, 5*s.*

—— *Sound Bodies for our Boys and Girls.* 16mo, 2*s.* 6*d.*

Bonwick. British Colonies. Asia, 1*s.*; Africa, 1*s.*; America, 1*s.*; Australasia, 1*s.* One vol., cloth, 5*s.*

Bosanquet (Rev. C.) Blossoms from the King's Garden: Sermons for Children. 2nd Edition, small post 8vo, cloth extra, 6*s.*

—— *Jehoshaphat; or, Sunlight and Clouds.* 1*s.*

Boussenard (L.) Crusoes of Guiana. Gilt, 2*s.* 6*d.*; gilt ed. 3*s.* 6*d.*

—— *Gold-seekers.* Sequel to the above. Illust. 16mo, 5*s.*

Boyesen (F.) Story of Norway. Illustrated, sm. 8vo, 7*s.* 6*d.*

Boyesen (H. H.) Modern Vikings: Stories of Life and Sport in Norseland. Cr. 8vo, 6*s.*

Boy's Froissart. King Arthur. Knightly Legends of Wales. Percy. See LANIER.

Bradshaw (J.) New Zealand of To-day, 1884-87. 8vo.

Brannt (W. T.) Animal and Vegetable Fats and Oils. 244 Illust., 8vo, 35*s.*

—— *Manufacture of Soap and Candles, with many Formulas.* Illust., 8vo, 35*s.*

—— *Metallic Alloys. Chiefly from the German of Krupp* and Wilberger. Crown 8vo, 12*s.* 6*d.*

Bright (John) Public Letters. Crown 8vo, 7*s.* 6*d.*

Brisse (Baron) Menus (366). A *menu,* in French and English, for every Day in the Year. 2nd Edition. Crown 8vo, 5*s.*

British Fisheries Directory. Small 8vo, 2*s.* 6*d.*

Brittany. See BLACKBURN.

Browne (G. Lennox) Voice Use and Stimulants. Sm. 8vo, 3*s.* 6*d.*

—— and *Behnke (Emil) Voice, Song, and Speech.* N ed., 5*s.*

Bryant (W. C.) and Gay (S. H.) History of the United States. 4 vols., royal 8vo, profusely Illustrated, 60*s.*

Bryce (Rev. Professor) Manitoba. Illust. Crown 8vo, 7*s.* 6*d.*

—— *Short History of the Canadian People.* 7*s.* 6*d.*

Burnaby (Capt.) On Horseback through Asia Minor. 2 vols., 8vo, 38*s.* Cheaper Edition, 1 vol., crown 8vo, 10*s.* 6*d.*

Burnaby (Mrs. F.) High Alps in Winter; or, Mountaineering in Search of Health. With Illustrations, &c., 14*s*. See also MAIN.
Burnley (J.) History of Wool and Woolcombing. Illust. 8vo, 21*s*.
Burton (Sir R. F.) Early, Public, and Private Life. Edited by F. HITCHMAN. 2 vols., 8vo, 36*s*.
Butler (Sir W. F.) Campaign of the Cataracts. Illust., 8vo, 18*s*.
—— *Invasion of England, told twenty years after.* 2*s*. 6*d*.
—— *Red Cloud; or, the Solitary Sioux.* Imperial 16mo, numerous illustrations, gilt edges, 3*s*. 6*d*.; plainer binding, 2*s*. 6*d*.
—— *The Great Lone Land; Red River Expedition.* 7*s*. 6*d*.
—— *The Wild North Land; the Story of a Winter Journey* with Dogs across Northern North America. 8vo, 18*s*. Cr. 8vo, 7*s*. 6*d*.

CABLE (G. W.) Bonaventure: A Prose Pastoral of Acadian Louisiana. Sm. post 8vo, 5*s*.
Cadogan (Lady A.) Illustrated Games of Patience. Twenty-four Diagrams in Colours, with Text. Fcap. 4to, 12*s*. 6*d*.
—— *New Games of Patience.* Coloured Diagrams, 4to, 12*s*.6*d*.
Caldecott (Randolph) Memoir. By HENRY BLACKBURN. With 170 Examples of the Artist's Work. 14*s*.; large paper, 21*s*.
California. See NORDHOFF.
Callan (H.) Wanderings on Wheel and on Foot. Cr. 8vo, 1*s*. 6*d*.
Campbell (Lady Colin) Book of the Running Brook: and of Still Waters. 5*s*.
Canadian People: Short History. Crown 8vo, 7*s*. 6*d*.
Carleton (Will) Farm Ballads, Farm Festivals, and Farm Legends. Paper boards, 1*s*. each; 1 vol., small post 8vo, 3*s*. 6*d*.
—— *City Ballads.* Illustrated, 12*s*. 6*d*. New Ed. (Rose Library), 16mo, 1*s*.
Carnegie (A.) American Four-in-Hand in Britain. Small 4to, Illustrated, 10*s*. 6*d*. Popular Edition, paper, 1*s*.
—— *Round the World.* 8vo, 10*s*. 6*d*.
—— *Triumphant Democracy.* 6*s*.; also 1*s*. 6*d*. and 1*s*.
Chairman's Handbook. By R. F. D. PALGRAVE. 5th Edit., 2*s*.
Changed Cross, &c. Religious Poems. 16mo, 2*s*. 6*d*.; calf, 6*s*.
Chaplin (J. G.) Three Principles of Book-keeping. 2*s*. 6*d*.
Charities of London. See Low's.
Chattock (R. S.) Practical Notes on Etching. New Ed. 8vo, 10*s*. 6*d*.
Chess. See BIRD (H. E.).

Children's Praises. Hymns for Sunday-Schools and Services.
Compiled by LOUISA H. H. TRISTRAM. 4*d.*

Choice Editions of Choice Books. 2*s.* 6*d.* each. Illustrated by C. W. COPE, R.A., T. CRESWICK, R.A., E. DUNCAN, BIRKET FOSTER, J. C. HORSLEY, A.R.A., G. HICKS, R. REDGRAVE, R A., C. STONEHOUSE, F. TAYLER, G. THOMAS, H. J. TOWNSHEND, E. H. WEHNERT, HARRISON WEIR, &c.

Bloomfield's Farmer's Boy.	Milton's L'Allegro.
Campbell's Pleasures of Hope.	Poetry of Nature. Harrison Weir.
Coleridge's Ancient Mariner.	Rogers' (Sam.) Pleasures of Memory.
Goldsmith's Deserted Village.	Shakespeare's Songs and Sonnets.
Goldsmith's Vicar of Wakefield.	Tennyson's May Queen.
Gray's Elegy in a Churchyard.	Elizabethan Poets.
Keat's Eve of St. Agnes.	Wordsworth's Pastoral Poems.

"Such works are a glorious beatification for a poet."—*Athenæum.*

Chreiman (Miss) Physical Culture of Women. A Lecture at the Parkes Museum. Small 8vo, 1*s.*

Christ in Song. By PHILIP SCHAFF. New Ed., gilt edges, 6*s.*

Chromo-Lithography. See AUDSLEY.

Cochran (W.) Pen and Pencil in Asia Minor. Illust., 8vo, 21*s.*

Collingwood (Harry) Under the Meteor Flag. The Log of a Midshipman. Illustrated, small post 8vo, gilt, 3*s.* 6*d.*; plainer, 2*s.* 6*d.*

—— *Voyage of the " Aurora."* Gilt, 3*s.* 6*d.* ; plainer, 2*s.* 6*d.*

Cook (Dutton) Book of the Play. New Edition. 1 vol., 3*s.* 6*d.*

—— *On the Stage: Studies.* 2 vols., 8vo, cloth, 24*s.*

Cowen (Jos., M.P.) Life and Speeches. 8vo, 14*s.*

Cowper (W.) Poetical Works: A Concordance. Roy. 8vo, 21*s.*

Cozzens (F.) American Yachts. 27 Plates, 22 × 28 inches. Proofs, £21 ; Artist's Proofs, £31 10*s.*

Crew (B. J.) Practical Treatise on Petroleum. Illust., 8vo, 28*s.*

Crouch (A. P.) On a Surf-bound Coast. Crown 8vo, 7*s.* 6*d.*

Crown Prince of Germany : a Diary. 2*s.* 6*d.*

Cudworth (W.) Life and Correspondence of Abraham Sharp. Illustrated from Drawings. (To Subscribers, 21*s.*) 26*s.*

Cumberland (Stuart) Thought Reader's Thoughts. Cr. 8vo., 10*s.* 6*d.*

—— *Queen's Highway from Ocean to Ocean.* Ill., 8vo, 18*s.* ; new ed., 7*s.* 6*d.*

Cundall (Joseph) Annals of the Life and Work of Shakespeare. With a List of Early Editions. 3*s.* 6*d.* ; large paper, 5*s.*; also 2*s.*

—— *Remarkable Bindings in the British Museum.*

Curtis (W. E.) Capitals of Spanish America.. Illust., roy. 8vo.

Cushing (W.) Initials and Pseudonyms. Large 8vo, 25*s.*; second series, large 8vo, 21*s.*

Custer (Eliz. B.) Tenting on the Plains; Gen. Custer in Kansas and Texas. Royal 8vo, 18s.
Cutcliffe (H. C.) Trout Fishing in Rapid Streams. Cr. 8vo, 3s. 6d.

DALY (Mrs. D.) Digging, Squatting, and Pioneering in Northern South Australia. 8vo, 12s.
D'Anvers. Elementary History of Art. New ed., 360 illus., cr. 8vo, 2 vols. (5s. each), gilt, 10s. 6d.
—— *Elementary History of Music.* Crown 8vo, 2s. 6d.
Davidson (H. C.) Old Adam; Tale of an Army Crammer. 3 vols. crown 8vo, 31s. 6d.
Davis (Clement) Modern Whist. 4s.
Davis (C. T.) Bricks, Tiles, Terra-Cotta, &c. Ill. 8vo, 25s.
—— *Manufacture of Leather.* With many Illustrations. 52s. 6d.
—— *Manufacture of Paper.* 28s.
Davis (G. B.) Outlines of International Law. 8vo. 10s. 6d.
Dawidowsky. Glue, Gelatine, Isinglass, Cements, &c. 8vo, 12s. 6d.
Day of My Life at Eton. By an ETON BOY. 16mo. 2s. 6d.
Day's Collacon: an Encyclopædia of Prose Quotations. Imperial 8vo, cloth, 31s. 6d.
De Leon (E.) Under the Stars and under the Crescent. N. ed., 6s.
Dethroning Shakspere. Letters to the Daily Telegraph; and Editorial Papers. Crown 8vo, 2s. 6d.
Dictionary. See TOLHAUSEN, "Technological."
Dogs in Disease. By ASHMONT. Crown 8vo, 7s. 6d.
Donnelly (Ignatius) Atlantis; or, the Antediluvian World. 7th Edition, crown 8vo, 12s. 6d.
—— *Ragnarok: The Age of Fire and Gravel.* Illustrated, crown 8vo, 12s. 6d.
—— *The Great Cryptogram: Francis Bacon's Cipher in the* so-called Shakspere Plays. With facsimiles. 2 vols., 30s.
Doré (Gustave) Life and Reminiscences. By BLANCHE ROOSEVELT. Illust. from the Artist's Drawings. Medium 8vo, 24s.
Dougall (James Dalziel) Shooting: its Appliances, Practice, and Purpose. New Edition, revised with additions. Crown 8vo, 7s. 6d.
"The book is admirable in every way. . . . . We wish it every success "—*Globe.*
"A very complete treatise. . Likely to take high rank as an authority on shooting "—*Daily News.*
Dupré (Giovanni). By FRIEZE. With Dialogues on Art. 7s. 6d.

EDMONDS (C.) Poetry of the Anti-Jacobin. With Additional matter. New ed. Illust., crown 8vo.
Educational List and Directory for 1887-88. 5s.

Educational Works published in Great Britain. A Classified Catalogue. Third Edition, 8vo, cloth extra, 6s.
Edwards (E.) American Steam Engineer. Illust., 12mo, 12s. 6d.
Eight Months on the Argentine Gran Chaco. 8vo, 8s. 6d.
Elliott (H. W.) An Arctic Province: Alaska and the Seal Islands. Illustrated from Drawings; also with Maps. 16s.
Emerson (Dr. P. H.) Pictures of East Anglian Life. Ordinary ed., 105s.; édit. de luxe, 17 × 13½, vellum, morocco back, 147s.
—— *Naturalistic Photography for Art Students.* Crown 8vo.
—— *and Goodall. Life and Landscape on the Norfolk Broads.* Plates 12 × 8 inches, 126s.; large paper, 210s.
English Catalogue of Books. Vol. III., 1872—1880. Royal 8vo, half-morocco, 42s. See also "Index."
English Etchings. Published Quarterly. 3s. 6d. Vol. VI., 25s.
English Philosophers. Edited by E. B. IVAN MÜLLER, M.A.
Crown 8vo volumes of 180 or 200 pp., price 3s. 6d. each.

Francis Bacon, by Thomas Fowler. | Shaftesbury and Hutcheson.
Hamilton, by W. H. S. Monck. | Adam Smith, by J. A. Farrer.
Hartley and James Mill. |

Esmarch (F.) Handbook of Surgery. Translation from the last German Edition. With 647 new Illustrations. 8vo, leather, 24s.
Etching. See CHATTOCK, and ENGLISH ETCHINGS.
Etchings (Modern) of Celebrated Paintings. 4to, 31s. 6d.
Evans (E. A.) Songs of the Birds. Analogies of Spiritual Life. New Ed. Illust., 6s.
Evelyn. Life of Mrs. Godolphin. By WILLIAM HARCOURT, of Nuneham. Steel Portrait. Extra binding, gilt top, 7s. 6d.

FARINI (G. A.) Through the Kalahari Desert. 8vo, 21s.
Farm Ballads, Festivals, and Legends. See CARLETON.
Fawcett (Edgar) A Gentleman of Leisure. 1s.
Fenn (G. Manville) Off to the Wilds: A Story for Boys. Profusely Illustrated. Crown 8vo, gilt edges, 3s. 6d.; plainer, 2s. 6d.
—— *Silver Cañon.* Illust., gilt ed., 3s. 6d.; plainer, 2s. 6d.
Fennell (Greville) Book of the Roach. New Edition, 12mo, 2s.
Ferns. See HEATH.
Field (H. M.) Greek Islands and Turkey after the War. 8s. 6d.
Field (Mrs. Horace) Anchorage. 2 vols., crown 8vo, 12s.
Fields (J. T.) Yesterdays with Authors. New Ed., 8vo, 10s. 6d.
Fitzgerald (P.) Book Fancier. Cr. 8vo. 5s.; large pap. 12s. 6d.

Fleming (Sandford) England and Canada : a Tour. Cr. 8vo, 6s.
Florence. See YRIARTE.
Folkard (R., Jun.) Plant Lore, Legends, and Lyrics. 8vo, 16s.
Forbes (H. O.) Naturalist in the Eastern Archipelago. 8vo. 21s.
Foreign Countries and British Colonies. Cr. 8vo, 3s. 6d. each.

Australia, by J. F. Vesey Fitzgerald.	Japan, by S. Mossman.
Austria, by D Kay, F.R G.S.	Peru, by Clements R. Markham.
Denmark and Iceland, by E. C. Otté.	Russia, by W. R. Morfill, M.A.
Egypt, by S. Lane Poole, B.A.	Spain, by Rev. Wentworth Webster.
France, by Miss M. Roberts.	Sweden and Norway, by Woods.
Germany, by S. Baring-Gould.	West Indies, by C. H. Eden,
Greece, by L. Sergeant, B.A.	F.R.G.S.

Foreign Etchings. From Paintings by Rembrandt, &c., 63s.; india proofs, 147s.
Fortunes made in Business. Vols. I., II., III. 16s. each.
Frampton (Mary) Journal, Letters, and Anecdotes. 8vo, 14s.
Franc (Maud Jeanne). Small post 8vo, uniform, gilt edges :—

Emily's Choice. 5s.	Vermont Vale. 5s.
Hall's Vineyard. 4s.	Minnie's Mission. 4s.
John's Wife: A Story of Life in South Australia. 4s.	Little Mercy. 4s.
	Beatrice Melton's Discipline. 4s.
Marian; or, The Light of Some One's Home. 5s.	No Longer a Child. 4s.
	Golden Gifts. 4s.
Silken Cords and Iron Fetters. 4s.	Two Sides to Every Question. 4s.
Into the Light. 4s.	Master of Ralston. 4s.

Also a Cheap Edition, in cloth extra, 2s. 6d. each.
Frank's Ranche; or, My Holiday in the Rockies. A Contribution to the Inquiry into What we are to Do with our Boys. 5s.
Freeman (J.) Lights and Shadows of Melbourne Life. Cr. 8vo. 6s.
French. See JULIEN and PORCHER.
Fresh Woods and Pastures New. By the Author of "An Amateur Angler's Days." 1s. 6d.; large paper, 5s. ; new ed., 1s.
Froissart. See LANIER.
Fuller (Edward) Fellow Travellers. 3s. 6d.
—— *Dramatic Year 1887-88 in the United States.* With the London Season, by W. ARCHER. Crown 8vo.

GANE (D. N.) New South Wales and Victoria in 1885. 5s.

Gasparin (Countess A. de) Sunny Fields and Shady Woods. 6s.
Geary (Grattan) Burma after the Conquest. 7s. 6d.
Gentle Life (Queen Edition). 2 vols. in 1, small 4to, 6s.

THE GENTLE LIFE SERIES.

Price 6s. each ; or in calf extra, price 10s. 6d. ; Smaller Edition, cloth extra, 2s. 6d., except where price is named.

The Gentle Life. Essays in aid of the Formation of Character.
About in the World. Essays by Author of " The Gentle Life."
Like unto Christ. New Translation of Thomas à Kempis.
Familiar Words. A Quotation Handbook. 6s.
Essays by Montaigne. Edited by the Author of " The Gentle Life."
The Gentle Life. 2nd Series.
The Silent Hour: Essays, Original and Selected.
Half-Length Portraits. Short Studies of Notable Persons. By J. HAIN FRISWELL.
Essays on English Writers, for Students in English Literature.
Other People's Windows. By J. HAIN FRISWELL. 6s.
A Man's Thoughts. By J. HAIN FRISWELL.
The Countess of Pembroke's Arcadia. By Sir PHILIP SIDNEY. 6s.

Germany. By S. BARING-GOULD. Crown 8vo, 3s. 6d.
Gibbon (C) Beyond Compare: a Story. 3 vols., cr. 8vo, 31s. 6d.
——— *Yarmouth Coast.*
Gisborne (W.) New Zealand Rulers and Statesmen. With Portraits. Crown 8vo, 7s. 6d.
Goldsmith. She Stoops to Conquer. Introduction by AUSTIN DOBSON ; the designs by E. A. ABBEY. Imperial 4to, 48s.
Goode (G. Brown) American Fishes. A Popular Treatise. Royal 8vo, 24s.
Gordon (J. E. H, B.A. Cantab.) Four Lectures on Electric Induction at the Royal Institution, 1878 9. Illust., square 16mo, 3s.
——— *Electric Lighting.* Illustrated, 8vo, 18s.
——— *Physical Treatise on Electricity and Magnetism.* 2nd Edition, enlarged, with coloured, full-page, &c., Illust. 2 vols., 8vo, 42s.
——— *Electricity for Schools.* Illustrated. Crown 8vo, 5s.
Gouffé (Jules) Royal Cookery Book. New Edition, with plates in colours, Woodcuts, &c., 8vo, gilt edges, 42s.
——— Domestic Edition, half-bound, 10s. 6d.
Grant (General, U.S.) Personal Memoirs. 2 vols., 8vo, 28s. Illustrations, Maps, &c 2 vols, 8vo, 28s.
Great Artists. See " Biographies."

Great Musicians. Edited by F. HUEFFER. A Series of Biographies, crown 8vo, 3s. each :—

Bach.	Mendelssohn.	Schubert.
English Church Composers. By BARRETT.	Mozart.	Schumann.
	Purcell.	Richard Wagner.
Handel.	Rossini.	Weber.
Haydn.		

Groves (J. Percy) Charmouth Grange. Gilt, 5s.; plainer, 2s. 6d.

Guizot's History of France. Translated by R. BLACK. In 8 vols., super-royal 8vo, cloth extra, gilt, each 24s. In cheaper binding, 8 vols., at 10s. 6d. each.

"It supplies a want which has long been felt, and ought to be in the hands of all students of history "—*Times.*

———————————— *Masson's School Edition.* Abridged from the Translation by Robert Black, with Chronological Index, Historical and Genealogical Tables, &c. By Professor GUSTAVE MASSON, B.A. With Portraits, Illustrations, &c. 1 vol., 8vo, 600 pp., 5s.

Guyon (Mde.) Life. By UPHAM. 6th Edition, crown 8vo, 6s.

HALFORD (F. M.) Floating Flies, and how to Dress them. Coloured plates. 8vo, 15s.; large paper, 30s.

—————— *Dry Fly-Fishing in Theory and Practice.* Col. Plates.

Hall (W. W.) How to Live Long; or, 1408 *Maxims.* 2s.

Hamilton (E.) Recollections of Fly-fishing for Salmon, Trout, and Grayling. With their Habits, Haunts, and History. Illust., 6s.; large paper, 10s. 6d.

Hands (T.) Numerical Exercises in Chemistry. Cr. 8vo, 2s. 6d. and 2s.; Answers separately, 6d.

Hardy (Thomas). See LOW'S STANDARD NOVELS.

Hare (J. S. Clark) Law of Contracts. 8vo, 26s.

Harley (T.) Southward Ho! to the State of Georgia. 5s.

Harper's Magazine. Published Monthly. 160 pages, fully Illustrated, 1s. Vols., half yearly, I.—XVI., super-royal 8vo, 8s. 6d. each.

"'Harper's Magazine' is so thickly sown with excellent illustrations that to count them would be a work of time; not that it is a picture magazine, for the engravings illustrate the text after the manner seen in some of our choicest *éditions de luxe.*"— *St James's Gazette.*

"It is so pretty, so big, and so cheap.... An extraordinary shillingsworth—160 large octavo pages, with over a score of articles, and more than three times as many illustrations "—*Edinburgh Daily Review.*

"An amazing shillingsworth ... combining choice literature of both nations."— *Nonconformist.*

Harper's Young People. Vols. I.-IV., profusely Illustrated with woodcuts and coloured plates. Royal 4to, extra binding, each 7s. 6d.; gilt edges, 8s. Published Weekly, in wrapper, 1d.; Annual Subscription, post free, 6s. 6d.; Monthly, in wrapper, with coloured plate, 6d.; Annual Subscription, post free, 7s. 6d.

Harrison (Mary) Skilful Cook. New edition, crown 8vo, 5s.
Hartshorne (H.) Household Medicine, Surgery, &c. 8vo. 21s.
Hatton (Frank) North Borneo. Map and Illust., &c. 18s.
Hatton (Joseph) Journalistic London: with Engravings and
    Portraits of Distinguished Writers of the Day. Fcap. 4to, 12s. 6d.
—————— See also LOW'S STANDARD NOVELS.
Hawthorne (Nathaniel) Life. By JOHN R. LOWELL.
Heath (Francis George) Fern World With Nature-printed
    Coloured Plates. Crown 8vo, gilt edges, 12s. 6d. Cheap Edition, 6s.
Heath (Gertrude). Tell us Why? The Customs and Ceremo-
    nies of the Church of England explained for Children. Cr. 8vo, 2s. 6d.
Heldmann (B) Mutiny of the Ship "Leander." Gilt edges,
    3s. 6d.; plainer, 2s. 6d.
Henty. Winning his Spurs. Cr. 8vo, 3s. 6d.; plainer, 2s. 6d.
—————— *Cornet of Horse.* Cr. 8vo, 3s. 6d.; plainer, 2s. 6d.
—————— *Jack Archer.* Illust. 3s. 6d.; plainer, 2s. 6d.
Henty (Richmond) Australiana : My Early Life. 5s.
Herrick (Robert) Poetry. Preface by AUSTIN DOBSON. With
    numerous Illustrations by E. A. ABBEY. 4to, gilt edges, 42s.
Hetley (Mrs. E.) Native Flowers of New Zealand. Chromos
    from Drawings. Three Parts, to Subscribers, 63s.
Hewitt (James A.) Church History in South Africa, 1795-1848,
    12mo, 5s.
Hicks (E. S.) Our Boys: How to Enter the Merchant Service. 5s.
—————— *Yachts, Boats and Canoes.* Illustrated. 8vo, 10s. 6d.
Hitchman. Public Life of the Earl of Beaconsfield. 3s. 6d.
Hoey (Mrs. Cashel) See LOW'S STANDARD NOVELS.
Hofmann. Scenes from the Life of our Saviour. 12 mounted
    plates, 12 × 9 inches, 21s.
Holder (C. F.) Marvels of Animal Life. Illustrated. 8s 6d.
—————— *Ivory King: Elephant and Allies.* Illustrated. 8s. 6d.
—————— *Living Lights: Phosphorescent Animals and Vegetables.*
    Illustrated. 8vo, 8s. 6d.
Holmes (O. W) Before the Curfew, &c. Occasional Poems. 5s.
—————— *Last Leaf : a Holiday Volume.* 42s.
—————— *Mortal Antipathy,* 8s. 6d.; also 2s.; paper, 1s.
—————— *Our Hundred Days in Europe.* 6s. Large Paper, 15s.
—————— *Poetical Works.* 2 vols., 18mo, gilt tops, 10s. 6d.
Homer, Iliad I.-XII., done into English Verse. By ARTHUR
    S. WAY. 9s.
—————— *Odyssey, done into English Verse.* By A. S. WAY.
    Fcap 4to, 7s. 6d.

Hopkins (Manley) Treatise on the Cardinal Numbers. 2s. 6d.

Hore (Mrs.) To Lake Tanganyika in a Bath Chair. Cr. 8vo, 7s. 6d.

Howard (Blanche W.) Tony the Maid; a Novelette. Illust., 12mo, 3s. 6d.

Howorth (H. H.) Mammoth and the Flood. 8vo, 18s.

Huet (C. B.) Land of Rubens. For Visitors to Belgium. By VAN DAM. Crown 8vo, 3s. 6d.

Hugo (V.) Notre Dame. With coloured etchings and 150 engravings. 2 vols. 8vo, vellum cloth, 30s.

Hunared Greatest Men (The). 8 portfolios, 21s. each, or 4 vols., half-morocco, gilt edges, 10 guineas. New Ed., 1 vol., royal 8vo, 21s.

Hutchinson (T.) Diary and Letters. Vol. I., 16s.; Vol. II., 16s.

Hygiene and Public Health. Edited by A. H. BUCK, M.D. Illustrated. 2 vols., royal 8vo, 42s.

Hymnal Companion to the Book of Common Prayer. By BISHOP BICKERSTETH. In various styles and bindings from 1d. to 31s. 6d. Price List and Prospectus will be forwarded on application.

Hymns and Tunes at St. Thomas', New York. Music by G. W. FARREN. Royal 8vo, 5s.

ILLUSTRATED Text-Books of Art-Education. Edited by EDWARD J. POYNTER, R.A. Illustrated, and strongly bound, 5s. Now ready:—

PAINTING.

Classic and Italian. By HEAD. | French and Spanish.
German, Flemish, and Dutch. | English and American.

ARCHITECTURE.

Classic and Early Christian.
Gothic and Renaissance. By T. ROGER SMITH.

SCULPTURE.

Antique: Egyptian and Greek.
Renaissance and Modern. By LEADER SCOTT.

Inderwick (F. A.; Q.C.) Side Lights on the Stuarts. Essays. Illustrated, 8vo.

Index to the English Catalogue, Jan., 1874, to Dec., 1880. Royal 8vo, half-morocco, 18s.

Inglis (Hon. James; "Maori") Our New Zealand Cousins. Small post 8vo, 6s.

—— *Tent Life in Tiger Land: Twelve Years a Pioneer* Planter. Col. plates, roy 8vo, 18s.

Irving (Henry) Impressions of America. 2 vols., 21s.; 1 vol., 6s.

Irving (Washington). Library Edition of his Works in 27 vols., Copyright, with the Author's Latest Revisions. "Geoffrey Crayon" Edition, large square 8vo. 12s. 6d. per vol. *See also* "Little Britain."

JAMES (C.) Curiosities of Law and Lawyers. 8vo, 7s. 6d.
Japan. See ANDERSON, ARTISTIC, AUDSLEY, also MORSE.
Jefferies (Richard) Amaryllis at the Fair. Small 8vo, 7s. 6d.
Jerdon (Gertrude) Key-hole Country. Illustrated. Crown 8vo, cloth, 2s.
Johnston (H. H.) River Congo, from its Mouth to Bolobo. New Edition, 8vo, 21s.
Johnstone (D. Lawson) Land of the Mountain Kingdom. Illust., crown 8vo.
Jones (Major) Heroes of Industry. Biographies with Portraits. 7s. 6d.
—— *Emigrants' Friend.* Guide to the U.S. N. Ed. 2s. 6d.
Julien (F.) English Student's French Examiner. 16mo, 2s.
—— *Conversational French Reader.* 16mo, cloth, 2s. 6d.
—— *French at Home and at School.* Book I., Accidence 2s.
—— *First Lessons in Conversational French Grammar.* 1s.
—— *Petites Leçons de Conversation et de Grammaire.* 3s.
—— *Phrases of Daily Use.* Limp cloth, 6d.
—— " *Petites Leçons* " and " *Phrases* " in one. 3s. 6d.

KARR (H. W. Seton) Shores and Alps of Alaska. 8vo, 16s.
Keats. Endymion. Illust. by W. ST. JOHN HARPER. Imp. 4to, gilt top, 42s.
Kempis (Thomas à) Daily Text-Book. Square 16mo, 2s. 6d.; interleaved as a Birthday Book, 3s. 6d.
Kent's Commentaries: an Abriagment for Students of American Law. By EDEN F. THOMPSON 10s. 6d.
Kerr (W. M.) Far Interior: Cape of Good Hope, across the Zambesi, to the Lake Regions. Illustrated from Sketches, 2 vols. 8vo, 32s.
Kershaw (S. W.) Protestants from France in their English Home. Crown 8vo, 6s.
King (Henry) Savage London; Riverside Characters, &c. Crown 8vo, 6s.
Kingston (W. H. G.) Works. Illustrated, 16mo, gilt edges, 3s. 6d.; plainer binding, plain edges, 2s. 6d. each.

Captain Mugford, or, Our Salt and Fresh Water Tutors.	Snow-Shoes and Canoes. Two Supercargoes.
Dick Cheveley.	With Axe and Rifle.
Heir of Kilfinnan.	

Kingsley (Rose) Children of Westminster Abbey : Studies in English History. 5s.

Knight (E. J.) Cruise of the " Falcon." New Ed. Cr. 8vo, 7s. 6d.

Knox (Col.) Boy Travellers on the Congo. Illus. Cr. 8vo, 7s. 6d.

Kunhardt (C. B.) Small Yachts: Design and Construction. 35s.

—— *Steam Yachts and Launches.* Illustrated. 4to, 16s.

LAMB (Charles) Essays of Elia. Illustrated by C. O. MURRAY. 6s.

Lanier's Works. Illustrated, crown 8vo, gilt edges, 7s. 6d. each.

Boy's King Arthur.
Boy's Froissart.
Boy's Knightly Legends of Wales.
Boy's Percy: Ballads of Love and Adventure, selected from the "Reliques."

Lansdell (H.) Through Siberia. 2 vols., 8vo, 30s.; 1 vol., 10s. 6d.

—— *Russia in Central Asia.* Illustrated. 2 vols., 42s.

—— *Through Central Asia; Russo-Afghan Frontier, &c.* 8vo, 12s.

Larden (W.) School Course on Heat. Second Ed., Illust. 5s.

Laurie (André) Selene Company, Limited. Crown 8vo, 7s. 6d.

Layard (Mrs. Granville) Through the West Indies. Small post 8vo, 2s. 6d.

Lea (H. C.). History of the Inquisition of the Middle Ages. 3 vols, 8vo, 42s.

Lemon (M.) Small House over the Water, and Stories. Illust. by Cruikshank, &c. Crown 8vo, 6s.

Leo XIII.: Life. By BERNARD O'REILLY. With Steel Portrait from Photograph, &c. Large 8vo, 18s.; *édit. de luxe*, 63s.

Leonardo da Vinci's Literary Works. Edited by Dr. JEAN PAUL RICHTER. Containing his Writings on Painting, Sculpture, and Architecture, his Philosophical Maxims, Humorous Writings, and Miscellaneous Notes on Personal Events, on his Contemporaries, on Literature, &c.; published from Manuscripts. 2 vols., imperial 8vo, containing about 200 Drawings in Autotype Reproductions, and numerous other Illustrations. Twelve Guineas.

Library of Religious Poetry. Best Poems of all Ages. Edited by SCHAFF and GILMAN. Royal 8vo, 21s.; cheaper binding, 10s. 6d.

Lindsay (W. S.) History of Merchant Shipping. Over 150 Illustrations, Maps, and Charts. In 4 vols., demy 8vo, cloth extra. Vols. 1 and 2, 11s. each; vols. 3 and 4, 14s. each. 4 vols., 50s.

Little (Archibald J.) Through the Yang-tse Gorges : Trade and Travel in Western China. New Edition. 8vo, 10s. 6d.

Little Britain, The Spectre Bridegroom, and *Legend of Sleepy Hollow*. By WASHINGTON IRVING. An entirely New *Édition de luxe*. Illustrated by 120 very fine Engravings on Wood, by Mr. J. D. COOPER. Designed by Mr. CHARLES O. MURRAY. Re-issue, square crown 8vo, cloth, 6s.

Longfellow. Maidenhood. With Coloured Plates. Oblong 4to, 2s. 6d.; gilt edges, 3s. 6d.

—— *Courtship of Miles Standish.* Illust. by BROUGHTON, &c. Imp. 4to, 21s.

—— *Nuremberg.* 28 Photogravures. Illum. by M. and A. COMEGYS. 4to, 31s. 6d.

Lowell (J. R.) Vision of Sir Launfal. Illustrated, royal 4to, 63s.

—— *Life of Nathaniel Hawthorne.* Small post 8vo,

Low's Standard Library of Travel and Adventure. Crown 8vo, uniform in cloth extra, 7s. 6d., except where price is given.
1. The Great Lone Land. By Major W. F. BUTLER, C.B.
2. The Wild North Land. By Major W. F. BUTLER, C.B.
3. How I found Livingstone. By H. M. STANLEY.
4. Through the Dark Continent. By H. M. STANLEY. 12s. 6d.
5. The Threshold of the Unknown Region. By C. R. MARKHAM. (4th Edition, with Additional Chapters, 10s. 6d.)
6. Cruise of the Challenger. By W. J. J. SPRY, R.N.
7. Burnaby's On Horseback through Asia Minor. 10s. 6d.
8. Schweinfurth's Heart of Africa. 2 vols., 15s.
9. Through America. By W. G. MARSHALL.
10 Through Siberia. Il. aud unabridged, 10s.6d. By H. LANSDELL.
11. From Home to Home. By STAVELEY HILL.
12. Cruise of the Falcon. By E. J. KNIGHT.
13. Through Masai Land. By JOSEPH THOMSON.
14. To the Central African Lakes. By JOSEPH THOMSON.
15. Queen's Highway. By STUART CUMBERLAND.

Low's Standard Novels. Small post 8vo, cloth extra, 6s. each, unless otherwise stated.
A Daughter of Heth. By W. BLACK.
In Silk Attire. By W. BLACK.
Kilmeny. A Novel. By W. BLACK.
Lady Silverdale's Sweetheart. By W. BLACK.
Sunrise. By W. BLACK.
Three Feathers. By WILLIAM BLACK.
Alice Lorraine. By R. D. BLACKMORE.
Christowell, a Dartmoor Tale. By R. D. BLACKMORE.
Clara Vaughan. By R. D. BLACKMORE.
Cradock Nowell. By R. D. BLACKMORE.
Cripps the Carrier. By R. D. BLACKMORE.
Erema; or, My Father's Sin. By R. D. BLACKMORE.
Lorna Doone. By R. D. BLACKMORE. 25th Edition.
Mary Anerley. By R. D. BLACKMORE.
Tommy Upmore. By R. D. BLACKMORE.

Low's Standard Novels—continued.

Bonaventure. By G. W. CABLE.
An English Squire. By Miss COLERIDGE.
Some One Else. By Mrs. B. M. CROKER.
Under the Stars and Stripes. By E. DE LEON.
Halfway. By Miss BETHAM-EDWARDS.
A Story of the Dragonnades. By Rev. E. GILLIAT, M.A.
A Laodicean. By THOMAS HARDY.
Far from the Madding Crowd. By THOMAS HARDY.
Mayor of Casterbridge. By THOMAS HARDY.
Pair of Blue Eyes. By THOMAS HARDY.
Return of the Native. By THOMAS HARDY.
The Hand of Ethelberta. By THOMAS HARDY.
The Trumpet Major. By THOMAS HARDY.
Two on a Tower. By THOMAS HARDY.
Old House at Sandwich. By JOSEPH HATTON.
Three Recruits. By JOSEPH HATTON.
A Golden Sorrow. By Mrs. CASHEL HOEY. New Edition.
A Stern Chase. By Mrs. CASHEL HOEY.
Out of Court. By Mrs. CASHEL HOEY.
Don John. By JEAN INGELOW.
John Jerome. By JEAN INGELOW. 5s
Sarah de Berenger. By JEAN INGELOW.
Adela Cathcart. By GEORGE MAC DONALD.
Guild Court. By GEORGE MAC DONALD.
Mary Marston. By GEORGE MAC DONALD.
Stephen Archer. New Ed. of "Gifts." By GEORGE MAC DONALD.
The Vicar's Daughter. By GEORGE MAC DONALD.
Orts. By GEORGE MAC DONALD.
Weighed and Wanting. By GEORGE MAC DONALD.
Diane. By Mrs. MACQUOID.
Elinor Dryden. By Mrs. MACQUOID.
My Lady Greensleeves. By HELEN MATHERS.
Spell of Ashtaroth. By DUFFIELD OSBORNE. 5s.
Alaric Spenceley. By Mrs. J. H. RIDDELL.
Daisies and Buttercups. By Mrs. J. H. RIDDELL.
The Senior Partner. By Mrs. J. H. RIDDELL.
A Struggle for Fame. By Mrs. J. H. RIDDELL.
Frozen Pirate. By W. CLARK RUSSELL.
Jack's Courtship. By W. CLARK RUSSELL.
John Holdsworth. By W. CLARK RUSSELL.
A Sailor's Sweetheart. By W. CLARK RUSSELL.
Sea Queen. By W. CLARK RUSSELL.
Watch Below. By W. CLARK RUSSELL.
Strange Voyage. By W. CLARK RUSSELL.
Wreck of the Grosvenor. By W. CLARK RUSSELL.
The Lady Maud. By W. CLARK RUSSELL.
Little Loo. By W. CLARK RUSSELL.
Bee-man of Orn. By FRANK R. STOCKTON.
My Wife and I. By Mrs. HARRIET B. STOWE.

Low's Standard Novels—continued.
>   The Late Mrs. Null. By FRANK R. STOCKTON.
>   Hundredth Man. By FRANK R. STOCKTON.
>   Old Town Folk. By Mrs. HARRIET B. STOWE.
>   We and our Neighbours. By Mrs. HARRIET B. STOWE.
>   Poganuc People, their Loves and Lives. By Mrs. STOWE.
>   Ulu: an African Romance. By JOSEPH THOMSON.
>   Ben Hur: a Tale of the Christ. By LEW. WALLACE.
>   Anne. By CONSTANCE FENIMORE WOOLSON.
>   East Angels. By CONSTANCE FENIMORE WOOLSON.
>   For the Major. By CONSTANCE FENIMORE WOOLSON. 5s.
>   French Heiress in her own Chateau.

Low's Series of Standard Books for Boys. With numerous
>   Illustrations, 2s. 6d.; gilt edges, 3s. 6d. each.
>   Dick Cheveley. By W. H. G. KINGSTON.
>   Heir of Kilfinnan. By W. H. G. KINGSTON.
>   Off to the Wilds. By G. MANVILLE FENN.
>   The Two Supercargoes. By W. H. G KINGSTON.
>   The Silver Cañon. By G. MANVILLE FENN.
>   Under the Meteor Flag. By HARRY COLLINGWOOD.
>   Jack Archer: a Tale of the Crimea. By G. A. HENTY
>   The Mutiny on Board the Ship Leander. By B. HELDMANN.
>   With Axe and Rifle on the Western Prairies. By W. H. G. KINGSTON.
>   Red Cloud, the Solitary Sioux: a Tale of the Great Prairie. By Col. Sir WM. BUTLER, K.C.B.
>   The Voyage of the Aurora. By HARRY COLLINGWOOD.
>   Charmouth Grange: a Tale of the 17th Century. By J. PERCY GROVES.
>   Snowshoes and Canoes. By W. H. G. KINGSTON.
>   The Son of the Constable of France. By LOUIS ROUSSELET.
>   Captain Mugford; or, Our Salt and Fresh Water Tutors. Edited by W. H. G. KINGSTON.
>   The Cornet of Horse, a Tale of Marlborough's Wars. By G. A. HENTY.
>   The Adventures of Captain Mago. By LEON CAHUN.
>   Noble Words and Noble Needs.
>   The King of the Tigers. By ROUSSELET.
>   Hans Brinker; or, The Silver Skates. By Mrs. DODGE.
>   The Drummer-Boy, a Story of the time of Washington. By ROUSSELET.
>   Adventures in New Guinea: The Narrative of Louis Tregance.
>   The Crusoes of Guiana. By BOUSSENARD.
>   The Gold Seekers. A Sequel to the Above. By BOUSSENARD.
>   Winning His Spurs, a Tale of the Crusades. By G. A. HENTY.
>   The Blue Banner. By LEON CAHUN.

Low's Pocket Encyclopædia: a Compendium of General Knowledge for Ready Reference. Upwards of 25,000 References, with Plates. New ed., imp. 32mo, cloth, marbled edges, 3s. 6d.; roan, 4s. 6d

Low's Handbook to London Charities. Yearly, cloth, 1s. 6d.; paper, 1s.

McCORMICK (R.). Voyages in the Arctic and Antarctic Seas in Search of Sir John Franklin, &c. With Maps and Lithos. 2 vols., royal 8vo, 52s. 6d.

Mac Donald (George). See LOW'S STANDARD NOVELS.

Macdowall (Alex. B.) Curve Pictures of London for the Social Reformer. 1s.

McGoun's Commercial Correspondence. Crown 8vo, 5s.

Macgregor (John) "Rob Roy" on the Baltic. 3rd Edition, small post 8vo, 2s. 6d.; cloth, gilt edges, 3s. 6d.

———— *A Thousand Miles in the "Rob Roy" Canoe.* 11th Edition, small post 8vo, 2s. 6d.; cloth, gilt edges, 3s. 6d.

———— *Voyage Alone in the Yawl "Rob Roy."* New Edition, with additions, small post 8vo, 5s.; 3s. 6d. and 2s. 6d.

Mackay (C.) Glossary of Obscure Words in Shakespeare. 21s.

Mackenzie (Sir Morell) Fatal Illness of Frederick the Noble. Crown 8vo, limp cloth, 2s. 6d.

Mackenzie (Rev. John) Austral Africa: Losing it or Ruling it? Illustrations and Maps. 2 vols., 8vo, 32s.

McLellan's Own Story: The War for the Union. Illust. 18s.

McMurdo (Edward) History of Portugal. 8vo, 21s.

Macquoid (Mrs.). See LOW'S STANDARD NOVELS.

Magazine. See ENGLISH ETCHINGS, HARPER.

Maginn (W.) Miscellanies. Prose and Verse. With Memoir. 2 vols., crown 8vo, 24s.

Main (Mrs.; Mrs. Fred Burnaby) High Life and Towers of Silence. Illustrated, square 8vo, 10s. 6d.

Manitoba. See BRYCE.

Manning (E. F.) Delightful Thames. Illustrated. 4to, fancy boards, 5s.

Markham (Clements R.) The Fighting Veres, Sir F. and Sir H. 8vo, 18s.

———— *War between Peru and Chili,* 1879-1881. Third Ed. Crown 8vo, with Maps, 10s. 6d.

———— See also "Foreign Countries," MAURY, and VERES.

Marshall (W. G.) Through America. New Ed., cr. 8vo, 7s. 6d.

Marston (W.) Eminent Recent Actors, Reminiscences Critical, &c. 2 vols. Crown 8vo, 21s.

Martin (J. W.) Float Fishing and Spinning in the Nottingham Style. New Edition. Crown 8vo, 2s. 6d.

Matthews (J. W., M.D.) Incwadi Yami: Twenty years in
South Africa. With many Engravings, royal 8vo, 14s.

Maury (Commander) Physical Geography of the Sea, and its
Meteorology. New Edition, with Charts and Diagrams, cr. 8vo, 6s.

—— *Life.* By his Daughter. Edited by Mr. CLEMENTS R.
MARKHAM. With portrait of Maury. 8vo, 12s. 6d.

Men of Mark: Portraits of the most Eminent Men of the Day.
Complete in 7 Vols., 4to, handsomely bound, gilt edges, 25s. each.

Mendelssohn Family (The), 1729—1847. From Letters and
Journals. Translated. New Edition, 2 vols., 8vo, 30s.

Mendelssohn. See also " Great Musicians."

Merrifield's Nautical Astronomy. Crown 8vo, 7s. 6d.

Merrylees (J.) Carlsbad and its Environs. 7s. 6d.; roan, 9s.

Milford (P.) Ned Stafford's Experiences in the United States. 5s.

Mills (J.) Alternative Elementary Chemistry. Illust., cr. 8vo.

—— *Alernative Course in Physics.*

Mitchell (D. G.; Ik. Marvel) Works. Uniform Edition,
small 8vo, 5s. each.

Bound together.	Reveries of a Bachelor.
Doctor Johns.	Seven Stories, Basement and Attic.
Dream Life.	Wet Days at Edgewood.
Out-of-Town Places.	

Mitford (Mary Russell) Our Village. With 12 full-page and 157
smaller Cuts. Cr. 4to, cloth, gilt edges, 21s.; cheaper binding, 10s. 6d.

Moffatt (W.) Land and Work; Depression, Agricultural and
Commercial. Crown 8vo, 5s.

Mohammed Benani: A Story of To-day. 8vo, 10s. 6d.

Mollett (J. W.) Illustrated Dictionary of Words used in Art and
Archæology. Illustrated, small 4to, 15s.

Moloney (Governor) Forestry of West Africa. 10s. 6d.

Money (E.) The Truth about America. New Edition. 2s. 6d.

Morlands, The. A Tale of Anglo-Indian Life. By Author of
" Sleepy Sketches." Crown 8vo, 6s.

Morley (Henry) English Literature in the Reign of Victoria.
2000th volume of the Tauchnitz Collection of Authors. 18mo, 2s. 6d.

Mormonism. See " Stenhouse."

Morse (E. S.) Japanese Homes and their Surroundings. With
more than 300 Illustrations. Re-issue, 10s. 6d.

Morten (Honnor) Sketches of Hospital Life. Cr. 8vo, sewed, 1s.

Morwood. Our Gipsies in City, Tent, and Van. 8vo, 18s.

Moxon (Walter) Pilocereus Senilis. Fcap. 8vo, gilt top, 3s. 6d.

Muller (E.) Noble Words and Noble Deeds. Illustrated, gilt
edges, 3s 6d.; plainer binding, 2s. 6d.

Murray (E. C. Grenville) Memoirs. By his widow. 2 vols.
Musgrave (Mrs.) Miriam. Crown 8vo.
Music. See "Great Musicians."

NAPOLEON and Marie Louise: Memoirs. By Madame DURAND. 7s. 6d.
Nethercote (C. B.) Pytchley Hunt. New Ed., cr. 8vo, 8s. 6d.
New Zealand. See BRADSHAW.
New Zealand Rulers and Statesmen. See GISBORNE.
Nicholls (J. H. Kerry) The King Country: Explorations in New Zealand. Many Illustrations and Map. New Edition, 8vo, 21s.
Nisbet (Hume) Life and Nature Studies. With Etching by C. O. MURRAY. Crown 8vo, 6s.
Nordhoff (C.) California, for Health, Pleasure, and Residence. New Edition, 8vo, with Maps and Illustrations, 12s. 6d.
Norman (C. B.) Corsairs of France. With Portraits. 8vo, 18s.
Northbrook Gallery. Edited by LORD RONALD GOWER. 36 Permanent Photographs. Imperial 4to, 63s.; large paper, 105s.
Nott (Major) Wild Animals Photographed and Described. 35s.
Nursery Playmates (Prince of). 217 Coloured Pictures for Children by eminent Artists. Folio, in coloured boards, 6s.
Nursing Record. Yearly, 8s.; half-yearly, 4s. 6d.; quarterly, 2s. 6d; weekly, 2d.

O'BRIEN (R. B.) Fifty Years of Concessions to Ireland. With a Portrait of T. Drummond. Vol. I., 16s., II., 16s.
Orient Line Guide Book. By W. J. LOFTIE. 5s.
Orvis (C. F.) Fishing with the Fly. Illustrated. 8vo, 12s. 6d.
Osborne (Duffield) Spell of Ashtaroth. Crown 8vo, 5s.
Our Little Ones in Heaven. Edited by the Rev. H. ROBBINS. With Frontispiece after Sir JOSHUA REYNOLDS. New Edition, 5s.
Owen (Douglas) Marine Insurance Notes and Clauses. New Edition, 14s.

PALLISER (Mrs.) A History of Lace. New Edition, with additional cuts and text. 8vo, 21s.
—— *The China Collector's Pocket Companion.* With upwards of 1000 Illustrations of Marks and Monograms. Small 8vo, 5s.
Parkin (J.) Antidotal Treatment of Epidemic Cholera. 3s. 6d.
—— *Epidemiology in the Animal and Vegetable Kingdom.* Part I., crown 8vo, 3s. 6d.; Part II., 3s. 6d.
—— *Volcanic Origin of Epidemics.* Popular Edition, crown 8vo, 2s.

Payne (T. O.) Solomon's Temple and Capitol, Ark of the Flood
and **Tabernacle** (four sections at 24*s.*), extra binding, 105*s.*
Pennell (H. Cholmondeley) Sporting Fish of Great Britain
15*s.* ; large paper, 30*s.*
—————— *Modern Improvements in Fishing-tackle.* Crown 8vo, 2*s.*
Perelaer (M. T. H.) Ran Away from the Dutch; Borneo, &c.
Illustrated, square 8vo, 7*s.* 6*d.*
Pharmacopœia of the United States of America. 8vo, 21*s.*
Philpot (H. J.) Diabetes Mellitus. Crown 8vo, 5*s.*
—————— *Diet System.* Tables. I. Diabetes; II. Gout;
III. Dyspepsia; IV. Corpulence. In cases, 1*s.* each.
Plunkett (Major G. T.) Primer of Orthographic Projection.
Elementary Solid Geometry. With Problems and Exercises. 2*s.* 6*d.*
Poe (E. A.) The Raven. Illustr. by DORÉ. Imperial folio, 63*s.*
Poems of the Inner Life. Chiefly Modern. Small 8vo, 5*s.*
Polar Expeditions. See MCCORMICK.
Porcher (A.) Juvenile French Plays. With Notes and a
Vocabulary. 18mo, 1*s.*
Porter (Admiral David D.) Naval History of Civil War.
Portraits, Plans, &c. 4to, 25*s.*
Porter (Noah) Elements of Moral Science. 10*s.* 6*d.*
Portraits of Celebrated Race-horses of the Past and Present
Centuries. with Pedigrees and Performances. 4 vols., 4to, 126*s.*
Powles (L. D.) Land of the Pink Pearl: Life in the Bahamas.
8vo, 10*s.* 6*d.*
Poynter (Edward J., R.A.). See " Illustrated Text-books."
Pritt (T. E.) North Country Flies. Illustrated from the
Author's Drawings. 10*s* 6*d.*
Publishers' Circular (The), and General Record of British and
Foreign Literature. Published on the 1st and 15th of every Month, 3*d.*
Pyle (Howard) Otto of the Silver Hand. Illustrated by the
Author. 8vo, 8*s.* 6*d.*

RAMBAUD. *History of Russia.* New Edition, Illustrated.
3 vols., 8vo, 21*s.*
Reber. History of Mediæval Art. Translated by CLARKE.
422 Illustrations and Glossary. 8vo, .
Redford (G.) Ancient Sculpture. New Ed. Crown 8vo, 10*s.* 6*d.*
Reed (Sir E. J., M.P.) and Simpson. Modern Ships of War.
Illust., royal 8vo, 10*s.* 6*d.*
Richards (W.) Aluminium: its History, Occurrence, &c.
Illustrated, crown 8vo, 12*s.* 6*d.*

Richter (Dr. Jean Paul) Italian Art in the National Gallery.
4to. Illustrated. Cloth gilt, £2 2s.; half-morocco, uncut, £2 12s. 6d.
────── See also LEONARDO DA VINCI.
Riddell (Mrs. J. H.) See LOW'S STANDARD NOVELS.
Robertson (Anne J.) Myself and my Relatives. New Edition, crown 8vo, 5s.
Robin Hood; Merry Adventures of. Written and illustrated by HOWARD PYLE. Imperial 8vo, 15s.
Robinson (Phil.) In my Indian Garden. New Edition, 16mo, limp cloth, 2s.
────── *Noah's Ark. Unnatural History.* Sm. post 8vo, 12s. 6d.
────── *Sinners and Saints: a Tour across the United States of* America, and Round them. Crown 8vo, 10s. 6d.
────── *Under the Punkah.* New Ed., cr. 8vo, limp cloth, 2s.
Rockstro (W. S.) History of Music. New Edition. 8vo, 14s.
Roland, The Story of. Crown 8vo, illustrated, 6s.
Rolfe (Eustace Neville) Pompeii, Popular and Practical. Cr. 8vo, 7s. 6d.
Rome and the Environs. With plans, 3s.
Rose (J.) Complete Practical Machinist. New Ed., 12mo, 12s. 6d.
────── *Key to Engines and Engine-running.* Crown 8vo, 8s. 6d.
────── *Mechanical Drawing.* Illustrated, small 4to, 16s.
────── *Modern Steam Engines.* Illustrated. 31s. 6d.
────── *Steam Boilers. Boiler Construction and Examination.* Illust., 8vo, 12s. 6d.
Rose Library. Each volume, 1s. Many are illustrated—
Little Women. By LOUISA M. ALCOTT.
Little Women Wedded. Forming a Sequel to "Little Women."
Little Women and Little Women Wedded. 1 vol., cloth gilt, 3s. 6d.
Little Men. By L. M. ALCOTT. Double vol., 2s.; cloth gilt, 3s. 6d.
An Old-Fashioned Girl. By LOUISA M. ALCOTT. 2s.; cloth, 3s. 6d.
Work. A Story of Experience. By L. M. ALCOTT. 3s. 6d.; 2 vols., 1s. each.
Stowe (Mrs. H. B.) The Pearl of Orr's Island.
────── **The Minister's Wooing.**
────── **We and our Neighbours.** 2s.; cloth gilt, 6s.
────── **My Wife and I.** 2s.
Hans Brinker; or, the Silver Skates. By Mrs. DODGE. Also 5s.
My Study Windows. By J. R. LOWELL.
The Guardian Angel. By OLIVER WENDELL HOLMES.
My Summer in a Garden. By C. D. WARNER.
Dred. By Mrs. BEECHER STOWE. 2s.; cloth gilt, 3s. 6d.
City Ballads. New Ed. 16mo. By WILL CARLETON.

List of Publications. 25

Rose Library (The)—continued.
  Farm Ballads. By WILL CARLETON. ⎫
  Farm Festivals. By WILL CARLETON. ⎬ 1 vol., cl., gilt ed., 3s. 6d.
  Farm Legends. By WILL CARLETON. ⎭
  The Rose in Bloom. By L. M. ALCOTT. 2s.; cloth gilt, 3s. 6d.
  Eight Cousins. By L. M. ALCOTT. 2s.; cloth gilt, 3s. 6d.
  Under the Lilacs. By L. M. ALCOTT. 2s.; also 3s. 6d.
  Undiscovered Country. By W. D. HOWELLS.
  Clients of Dr. Bernagius. By L. BIART. 2 parts.
  Silver Pitchers. By LOUISA M. ALCOTT. Cloth, 3s. 6d.
  Jimmy's Cruise in the "Pinafore," and other Tales. By LOUISA M. ALCOTT. 2s.; cloth gilt, 3s. 6d.
  Jack and Jill. By LOUISA M. ALCOTT. 2s.; Illustrated, 5s.
  Hitherto. By the Author of the "Gayworthys." 2 vols., 1s. each; 1 vol., cloth gilt, 3s. 6d.
  A Gentleman of Leisure. A Novel. By EDGAR FAWCETT. 1s.

Ross (Mars) and Stonehewer Cooper. Highlands of Cantabria; or, Three Days from England. Illustrations and Map, 8vo, 21s.

Rothschilds, the Financial Rulers of Nations. By JOHN REEVES. Crown 8vo, 7s. 6d.

Rousselet (Louis) Son of the Constable of France. Small post 8vo, numerous Illustrations, gilt edges, 3s. 6d.; plainer, 2s. 6d.

—— *King of the Tigers: a Story of Central India.* Illustrated. Small post 8vo, gilt, 3s. 6d.; plainer, 2s. 6d.

—— *Drummer Boy.* Illustrated. Small post 8vo, gilt edges, 3s. 6d.; plainer, 2s. 6d.

Russell (Dora) Strange Message. 3 vols., crown 8vo, 31s. 6d.

Russell (W. Clark) Jack's Courtship. New Ed., small post 8vo, 6s.

—— *English Channel Ports and the Estate of the East* and West India Dock Company. Crown 8vo, 1s.

—— *Frozen Pirate.* New Ed., Illust., small post 8vo, 6s.

—— *Sailor's Language.* Illustrated. Crown 8vo, 3s. 6d.

—— *Sea Queen.* New Ed., small post 8vo, 6s.

—— *Strange Voyage.* New Ed., small post 8vo, 6s.

—— *The Lady Maud.* New Ed., small post 8vo, 6s.

—— *Wreck of the Grosvenor.* Small post 8vo, 6s. 4to, sewed, 6d.

*S*AINTS *and their Symbols: A Companion in the Churches* and Picture Galleries of Europe. Illustrated. Royal 16mo, 3s. 6d.

Samuels (Capt. J. S.) From Forecastle to Cabin: Autobiography. Illustrated. Crown 8vo, 8s. 6d.; also with fewer Illustrations, cloth. 2s.; paper, 1s.

Sandlands (J. P.) How to Develop Vocal Power. 1s.

Saunders (A.) Our Domestic Birds: Poultry in England and New Zealand. Crown 8vo, 6s.

―――― *Our Horses: the Best Muscles controlled by the Best* Brains. 6s.

Scherr (Prof. J.) History of English Literature. Cr. 8vo, 8s. 6d.

Schley. Rescue of Greely. Maps and Illustrations, 8vo, 12s 6d.

Schuyler (Eugène) American Diplomacy and the Furtherance of Commerce. 12s. 6d.

―――― *The Life of Peter the Great.* 2 vols., 8vo, 32s.

Schweinfurth (Georg) Heart of Africa. 2 vols., crown 8vo, 15s.

Scott (Leader) Renaissance of Art in Italy. 4to, 31s. 6d.

―――― *Sculpture, Renaissance and Modern.* 5s.

Semmes (Adm. Raphael) Service Afloat: The "Sumter" and the "Alabama." Illustrated. Royal 8vo, 16s.

Senior (W.) Near and Far: an Angler's Sketches of Home Sport and Colonial Life. Crown 8vo, 6s.

―――― *Waterside Sketches.* Imp. 32mo, 1s. 6d.; boards, 1s.

Shakespeare. Edited by R. GRANT WHITE. 3 vols., crown 8vo, gilt top, 36s.; *édition de luxe*, 6 vols., 8vo, cloth extra, 63s.

―――― See also CUNDALL, DETHRONING, DONNELLY, MACKAY, and WHITE (R. GRANT).

Shakespeare's Heroines: Studies by Living English Painters. 105s.; artists' proofs, 630s.

―――― *Songs and Sonnets.* Illust. by Sir JOHN GILBERT, R.A. 4to, boards, 5s.

Sharpe (R. Bowdler) Birds in Nature. 39 coloured plates and text. 4to, 63s.

Sidney (Sir Philip) Arcadia. New Edition, 6s.

Siegfried, The Story of. Illustrated, crown 8vo, cloth, 6s.

Simon. China: its Social Life. Crown 8vo, 6s.

Simson (A.) Wilds of Ecuador and Exploration of the Putumayor River. Crown 8vo, 8s. 6d.

Sinclair (Mrs.) Indigenous Flowers of the Hawaiian Islands. 44 Plates in Colour. Imp. folio, extra binding, gilt edges, 31s. 6d.

Sloane (T. O.) Home Experiments in Science for Old and Young. Crown 8vo, 6s.

Smith (G.) Assyrian Explorations. Illust. New Ed., 8vo, 18s.

―――― *The Chaldean Account of Genesis.* With many Illustrations. 16s. New Ed. By PROFESSOR SAYCE. 8vo, 18s.

Smith (G. Barnett) William I. and the German Empire. New Ed., 8vo, 3s. 6d.

Smith (J. Moyr) Wooing of Æthra. Illustrated. 32mo, 1s.

Smith (Sydney) Life and Times. By STUART J. REID. Illustrated. 8vo, 21s.

Smith (W. R.) Laws concerning Public Health. 8vo, 31s. 6d.

Spiers' French Dictionary. 29th Edition, remodelled. 2 vols., 8vo, 18s ; half bound, 21s.

Spry (W. J. J., R.N., F.R.G.S.) Cruise of H.M.S." Challenger." With Illustrations. 8vo, 18s. Cheap Edit., crown 8vo, 7s. 6d.

Spyri (Joh.) Heidi's Early Experiences: a Story for Children and those who love Children. Illustrated, small post 8vo, 4s. 6d.

—————— *Heidi's Further Experiences.* Illust., sm. post 8vo, 4s. 6d.

Stanley (H. M.) Congo, and Founding its Free State. Illustrated, 2 vols., 8vo, 42s. ; re-issue, 2 vols. 8vo, 21s.

—————— *How I Found Livingstone.* 8vo, 10s. 6d. ; cr. 8vo, 7s. 6d.

—————— *Through the Dark Continent.* Crown 8vo, 12s. 6d.

Start (J. W. K.) Junior Mensuration Exercises. 8d.

Stenhouse (Mrs.) Tyranny of Mormonism. An Englishwoman in Utah. New ed., cr. 8vo, cloth elegant, 3s. 6d.

Sterry (J. Ashby) Cucumber Chronicles. 5s.

Stevens (E. W.) Fly-Fishing in Maine Lakes. 8s. 6d.

Stevens (T.) Around the World on a Bicycle. Vol. II. 8vo. 16s.

Stockton (Frank R.) Rudder Grange. 3s. 6d.

—————— *Bee-Man of Orn, and other Fanciful Tales.* Cr. 8vo, 5s.

—————— *The Casting Away of Mrs. Lecks and Mrs. Aleshine.* 1s.

—————— *The Dusantes.* Sequel to the above. Sewed, 1s., this and the preceding book in one volume, cloth, 2s. 6d.

—————— *The Hundredth Man.* Small post 8vo, 6s.

—————— *The Late Mrs. Null.* Small post 8vo, 6s.

—————— *The Story of Viteau.* Illust. Cr. 8vo, 5s.

—————— See also LOW'S STANDARD NOVELS.

Stoker (Bram) Under the Sunset. Crown 8vo, 6s.

Storer (Professor F. H.) Agriculture in its Relations to Chemistry. 2 vols., 8vo, 25s.

Stowe (Mrs. Beecher) Dred. Cloth, gilt edges, 3s. 6d.; cloth, 2s.

—————— *Flowers and Fruit from her Writings.* Sm. post 8vo, 3s. 6d.

—————— *Little Foxes.* Cheap Ed., 1s.; Library Edition, 4s. 6d.

—————— *My Wife and I.* Cloth, 2s.

Stowe (*Mrs. Beecher*) *Old Town Folk.* 6s.

——— *We and our Neighbours.* 2s.

——— *Poganuc People.* 6s.

——— See also ROSE LIBRARY.

Strachan (*J.*) *Explorations and Adventures in New Guinea.* Illust., crown 8vo, 12s.

Stuttfield (*Hugh E. M.*) *El Maghreb*: 1200 *Miles' Ride through Marocco.* 8s. 6d.

Sullivan (*A. M.*) *Nutshell History of Ireland.* Paper boards, 6d.

*T*AINE (*H. A.*) "*Origines.*" Translated by JOHN DURAND.
    I. **The Ancient Regime.** Demy 8vo, cloth, 16s.
    II. **The French Revolution.** Vol. 1. do.
    III. Do. do. Vol. 2. do.
    IV. Do. do. Vol. 3. do.

Tauchnitz's English Editions of German Authors. Each volume, cloth flexible, 2s.; or sewed, 1s. 6d. (Catalogues post free.)

Tauchnitz (*B.*) *German Dictionary.* 2s.; paper, 1s. 6d.; roan, 2s. 6d.

——— *French Dictionary.* 2s.; paper, 1s. 6d.; roan, 2s. 6d.

——— *Italian Dictionary.* 2s.; paper, 1s. 6d.; roan, 2s. 6d.

——— *Latin Dictionary.* 2s.; paper, 1s. 6d.; roan, 2s. 6d.

——— *Spanish and English.* 2s.; paper, 1s. 6d.; roan, 2s 6d.

——— *Spanish and French.* 2s.; paper, 1s. 6d.; roan, 2s. 6d.

Taylor (*R. L.*) *Chemical Analysis Tables.* 1s.

——— *Chemistry for Beginners.* Small 8vo, 1s. 6d.

Techno-Chemical Receipt Book. With additions by BRANNT and WAHL. 10s. 6d.

Technological Dictionary. See TOLHAUSEN.

Thausing (*Prof.*) *Malt and the Fabrication of Beer.* 8vo, 45s.

Theakston (*M.*) *British Angling Flies.* Illustrated. Cr. 8vo, 5s.

Thomson (*Jos.*) *Central African Lakes.* New edition, 2 vols. in one, crown 8vo, 7s. 6d.

——— *Through Masai Land.* Illust. 21s.; new edition, 7s. 6d.

——— *and Miss Harris-Smith. Ulu: an African Romance.* crown 8vo, 6s.

Thomson (W.) Algebra for Colleges and Schools. With Answers, 5*s.* ; without, 4*s.* 6*d.* ; Answers separate, 1*s.* 6*d*

Tolhausen. Technological German, English, and French Dictionary. Vols. I., II., with Supplement, 12*s.* 6*d.* each ; III., 9*s.*; Supplement, cr. 8vo, 3*s.* 6*d.*

Tromholt (S.) Under the Rays of the Aurora Borealis. By C. SIEWERS. Photographs and Portraits. 2 vols., 8vo, 30*s.*

Tucker (W. J.) Life and Society in Eastern Europe. 15*s.*

Tupper (Martin Farquhar) My Life as an Author. 14*s.*

Turner (Edward) Studies in Russian Literature. Cr. 8vo, 8*s.* 6*d.*

UPTON (H.) Manual of Practical Dairy Farming. Cr. 8vo, 2*s.*

VAN DAM. Land of Rubens ; a companion for visitors to Belgium. See HUET.

Vane (Denzil) From the Dead. A Romance. 2 vols., cr. 8vo, 12*s.*

Vane (Sir Harry Young). By Prof. JAMES K. HOSMER. 8vo, 18*s.*

Veres. Biography of Sir Francis Vere and Lord Vere, leading Generals in the Netherlands. By CLEMENTS R. MARKHAM. 8vo, 18*s.*

Victoria (Queen) Life of. By GRACE GREENWOOD. Illust. 6*s.*

Vincent (Mrs. Howard) Forty Thousand Miles over Land and Water. With Illustrations. New Edit., 3*s.* 6*d.*

Viollet-le-Duc (E.) Lectures on Architecture. Translated by BENJAMIN BUCKNALL, Architect. 2 vols., super-royal 8vo, £3 3*s.*

WAKEFIELD. Aix-les-Bains : Bathing and Attractions. 6*d.*

Walford (Mrs. L. B.) Her Great Idea, and other Stories. Cr. 8vo, 10*s.* 6*d.*

Wallace (L.) Ben Hur : A Tale of the Christ. New Edition, crown 8vo, 6*s.* ; cheaper edition, 2*s.*

Waller (Rev. C. H.) The Names on the Gates of Pearl, and other Studies. New Edition. Crown 8vo, cloth extra, 3*s.* 6*d.*

—— *Words in the Greek Testament.* Part I. Grammar. Small post 8vo, cloth, 2*s.* 6*d.* Part II. Vocabulary, 2*s.* 6*d.*

BOOKS BY JULES VERNE.

WORKS. (Large Crown 8vo.)	Containing 350 to 600 pp. and from 50 to 100 full-page illustrations.		Containing the whole text with some illustr.	
	In very handsome cloth binding, gilt edges.	In plainer binding, plain edges.	In cloth binding, gilt edges, smaller type.	Coloured
	s. d.	s. d.	s. d.	
20,000 Leagues under the Sea. Parts I. and II.	10 6	8 0	3 6	2 vols., 1s.
Hector Servadac	10 6	0 0	3 6	2 vols., 1s.
The Fur Country	10 6	0 0	3 6	2 vols., 1s.
The Earth to the Moon and a Trip round it	10 6	0	2 vols., 2s. ea.	2 vols., 1s.
Michael Strogoff	10 6	0 0	3 6	2 vols., 1s.
Dick Sands, the Boy Captain	10 6	0 0	3 6	2 vols., 1s.
Five Weeks in a Balloon	7 6		2 0	1s.
Adventures of Three Englishmen and Three Russians	7 6	6	2 0	1 0
Round the World in Eighty Days	7 6	6	2 0	1 0
A Floating City	7 6	6		1 0
The Blockade Runners		6		1 0
Dr. Ox's Experiment	—	—		1 0
A Winter amid the Ice	—	—		1 0
Survivors of the "Chancellor"	7 6	3 6		2 vols., 1s.
Martin Paz				1s. 0
The Mysterious Island, 3 vols.:—	22 6	10 6	3 0	
I. Dropped from the Clouds	7 6	3 6	1 0	
II. Abandoned		3	1 0	
III. Secret of the Island		3	1 0	
The Child of the Cavern		3	1 0	
The Begum's Fortune		3	1 0	
The Tribulations of a Chinaman		3	1 0	
The Steam House, 2 vols.:				
I. Demon of Cawnpore	7 6	3 6	2 0	1 0
II. Tigers and Traitors	7 6	3 6	2 0	1 0
The Giant Raft, 2 vols.:—				
I. 800 Leagues on the Amazon	7 6	3 6	2 0	1 0
II. The Cryptogram	7 6	3 6	2 0	1 0
The Green Ray				
Godfrey Morgan			2 0	
Kéraban the Inflexible:—				
I. Captain of the "Guidara"	7 6	3 6	2 0	1 0
II. Scarpante the Spy	7 6	3 6	2 0	1 0
The Archipelago on Fire	7			
The Vanished Diamond	7			
Mathias Sandorf	10	5 0		
The Lottery Ticket	7			
Clipper of the Clouds	7			
North against South	7			
Adrift in the Pacific	7			
Flight to France	7			

Celebrated Travels and Travellers. 3 vols., 8vo, 600 pp., 100 full-page illustrations, gilt edges, 14s. each:—(1) The Exploration of the World. (2) The Great Navigators Eighteenth Century. (3) The Great Explorers of the Nineteenth Century.

Waller (Rev. C.H.) Adoption and the Covenant. On Confirmation. 2s. 6d.

—— *Silver Sockets; and other Shadows of Redemption.* Sermons at Christ Church, Hampstead. Small post 8vo, 6s.

Walsh (A. S.) Mary, Queen of the House of David. 8vo, 3s. 6d.

Walton (Iz.) Wallet Book, CIƆIƆLXXXV. Crown 8vo, half vellum, 21s.; large paper, 42s.

—— *Compleat Angler.* Lea and Dove Edition. Ed. by R. B. MARSTON. With full-page Photogravures on India paper, and the Woodcuts on India paper from blocks. 4to, half-morocco, 105s.; large paper, royal 4to, full dark green morocco, gilt top, 210s.

Walton (T. H.) Coal Mining. With Illustrations. 4to, 25s.

Wardrop (O.) Kingdom of Georgia. Illust. and map. 8vo. 14s.

Warner (C. D.) My Summer in a Garden. Boards, 1s.; leatherette, 1s. 6d.; cloth, 2s.

—— *Their Pilgrimage.* Illustrated by C. S. REINHART. 8vo, 7s. 6d.

Warren (W. F.) Paradise Found; the North Pole the Cra'le of the Human Race. Illustrated. Crown 8vo, 12s. 6d.

Washington Irving's Little Britain. Square crown 8vo, 6s.

Wells (H. P.) American Salmon Fisherman. 6s.

—— *Fly Rods and Fly Tackle.* Illustrated. 10s. 6d.

Wells (J. W.) Three Thousand Miles through Brazil. Illustrated from Original Sketches. 2 vols. 8vo, 32s.

Wenzel (O.) Directory of Chemical Products of the German Empire. 8vo, 25s.

White (R. Grant) England Without and Within. Crown 8vo, 10s. 6d.

—— *Every-day English.* 10s. 6d.

—— *Fate of Mansfield Humphreys, &c.* Crown 8vo, 6s.

—— *Studies in Shakespeare.* 10s. 6d.

—— *Words and their Uses.* New Edit., crown 8vo, 5s.

Whitney (Mrs.) The Other Girls. A Sequel to "We Girls." New ed. 12mo, 2s.

—— *We Girls.* New Edition. 2s.

Whittier (J. G.) The King's Missive, and later Poems. 18mo, choice parchment cover, 3s. 6d.

—— *St. Gregory's Guest, &c.* Recent Poems. 5s.

Wilcox (Marrion) Real People. Sm. post 8vo, 3s. 6d.

—— *Señora Villena; and Gray, an Oldhaven Romance.* 2 vols. in one, 6s.

William I. and the German Empire. By G. BARNETT SMITH. New Edition, 3s. 6d.

Willis-Bund (J.) Salmon Problems. 3s. 6d.; boards, 2s. 6d.

Wills (Dr. C. J.) Persia as it is. Crown 8vo, 8s. 6d.

Wills, A Few Hints on Proving, without Professional Assistance. By a PROBATE COURT OFFICIAL. 8th Edition, revised, with Forms of Wills, Residuary Accounts, &c. Fcap. 8vo, cloth limp, 1s.

Wilmot (A.) Poetry of South Africa. Collected and arranged. 8vo, 6s.

Wilson (Dr. Andrew) Health for the People. Cr. 8vo, 7s. 6d.

Winsor (Justin) Narrative and Critical History of America. 8 vols., 30s. each; large paper, per vol., 63s.

Woolsey. Introduction to International Law. 5th Ed., 18s.

Woolson (Constance F.) See "Low's Standard Novels."

Wright (H.) Friendship of God. Portrait, &c. Crown 8vo, 6s.

Wright (T.) Town of Cowper, Olney, &c. 6s.

Written to Order; the Journeyings of an Irresponsible Egotist. By the Author of "A Day of my Life at Eton." Crown 8vo, 6s.

YRIARTE (Charles) Florence: its History. Translated by C. B. PITMAN. Illustrated with 500 Engravings. Large imperial 4to, extra binding, gilt edges, 63s.; or 12 Parts, 5s. each.
History; the Medici; the Humanists; letters; arts; the Renaissance; illustrious Florentines; Etruscan art; monuments; sculpture; painting.

London:

SAMPSON LOW, MARSTON, SEARLE, & RIVINGTON, LD.,

St. Dunstan's House,

FETTER LANE, FLEET STREET, E.C.

RETURN TO the circulation desk of any
University of California Library

or to the

NORTHERN REGIONAL LIBRARY FACILITY
Bldg. 400, Richmond Field Station
University of California
Richmond, CA 94804-4698

ALL BOOKS MAY BE RECALLED AFTER 7 DAYS

- 2-month loans may be renewed by calling (510) 642-6753
- 1-year loans may be recharged by bringing books to NRLF
- Renewals and recharges may be made 4 days prior to due date

DD20 6M 9-03

FORM NO. DD6, UNIVERSITY OF CALIFORNIA, BERKELEY
BERKELEY, CA 94720